ABOUT THE AUTHOR

PHYLLIS PICKARD trained to teach at the Froebel Institute. Her first post at a pioneer school was at the Caldecott Community and she then went on to become joint head of Lawrence House School in London, where she was responsible for the curriculum of many gifted children. When the war came she studied under Professor Sir Cyril Burt and Professor J. C. Flugel, taking her BA in psychology and being awarded an MA for research on personality. After the war Miss Pickard spent eleven years on the staff of the Froebel Institute (for two of them she was seconded to Germany to lecture on child psychology), then ten years at Maria Grey College, the second half of this time as head of graduate training for primary teaching. She is a founder member of the National Association for Gifted Children and is author of several books, including *The Activity of Children, The Psychology of Developing Children* and (with C. Obrist) *Time for Reading*.

IF YOU THINK
YOUR CHILD
IS GIFTED

Other books by the same author

I Could a Tale Unfold
The Activity of Children
Time for Reading (with C. Obrist)
The Psychology of Developing Children

IF YOU THINK YOUR CHILD IS GIFTED

P. M. PICKARD

LINNET BOOKS
Hamden, Connecticut

First published in 1976
by George Allen & Unwin Ltd., London
and in the United States of America as a Linnet Book
an imprint of The Shoe String Press, Inc., Hamden
Connecticut 06514

© *Phyllis Pickard 1976*

ISBN 0-208-01583-3

Printed in Great Britain

To My Late Husband
Christopher Bailey

Acknowledgements

I should like to express my gratitude to all the people who have helped in the writing of this book. Just a few must be mentioned individually: Lord Redcliffe-Maud, GCR, CBE, Master of University College, Oxford, who kindly looked at the figures in Table 4 and encouraged me to use them; Brian Gardner, whose book *The Public Schools* was invaluable for parts of Chapter 2; the four artists who spared time to give their views on detecting and fostering talent in young children: Arnold Haskell on Ballet, Michal Hambourg on Music, Muriel Judd on Drama, and Bernard Ollis on Painting; the BBC for the broadcast of the Tenth Anniversary of the Yehudi Menuhin School; and Anthony Brackenbury, the school's headmaster, for saying something of the running of the school; my many friends in the United Kingdom National Association for Gifted Children, and particularly the Director, Henry Collis; my friend and colleague in the United States, first met through the World Organisation for Early Childhood Education (OMEP), Professor May V. Seagoe, who airmailed to me the Technical Report on thirteen PhD researches on gifted children as soon as it appeared. Last and most important, the long-suffering parents of the lively, gifted and talented children described in Chapter 5.

Contents

Tables

I

INTRODUCTION

Most people will have occasionally heard or seen or read in the newspapers of at least one or two exceptionally gifted children. Actual names are usually disguised, unless a child happens to have been billed for some public performance. From time to time people may hear privately of a gifted child, although it is rare to meet one. Let us consider some examples. One such child is a girl who used to have to wait, after her classmates had gone home, for her bus. Her home was cultured but not at all musical. One day she startled her parents by singing the first scene of *The Mikado* while in the bath. When there was a pause they went in to applaud, but the child, oblivious to the fact that the bath water was already cold, regarded them as an interruption as she had planned to sing the whole opera from start to finish. There was no Gilbert and Sullivan in the house, but how she had come to hear the opera can be explained. Her senior school was just coming up to the final rehearsal of their school production of *The Mikado*. While waiting for her bus she had heard bits and pieces of it, in odd order, many times. But it is not so easy to explain how she could work out the correct sequence, which she had never heard, and recall so much. She did later sing the whole opera to her parents, covering all the parts herself.

Another interesting case was a boy of three who pestered his mother to explain how reading is done. It is unusual for so young a child even to think that you actually do something to read. The mother, troubled by all she had read in the newspapers and magazines about not interfering with the schools' system of teaching reading, reluctantly promised to explain when he was four, rather hoping he would forget. He did not forget. The day he was four he reminded her of this promise. After tea she spent ten minutes explaining. He took the book away and from that moment read to himself. From time to time in the next four weeks he asked her to clarify some point which seemed incompatible with her explanation. Like Madame Curie, he had virtually taught himself to read when he was three. The brief explanation had fallen upon prepared ground. The mother very wisely did not tell her neighbours because their children were taking many months and even years to learn to read. To them this would seem like a very unfair distribution of gifts.

Another quick reader, this time a boy of five, appeared to be heading for disaster. Each day, before setting off for school, he read the leaders in the *Guardian* and *The Times* 'to compare their view points' as he explained. One should note that the boy belonged to a home which took both the *Guardian* and *The Times*, and one can well imagine the parents' reply when he had asked why they took two daily papers. The mother was looking forward to her son's first school Open Day, as he had not said much about what they did in school. She found him sitting motionless before an open introductory reader. As soon as she could get near him, she whispered, 'Don't they know you can read?' He tugged at her skirt and said that she was not to tell. In genuine astonishment, she asked how he passed the time. 'It is quite all right,' he whispered tensely, 'I take the first and the last word on every page, and make up a story for myself.' Once more he begged her not to tell. When he had gone to bed that night, the mother told the father. There was one of those emotional explosions known to most close-knit families. They disagreed about what steps to take. The father wanted to go roaring down in the morning to say what he thought of teachers who did not find out what their pupils knew. The mother, probably quite rightly, thought this might ruin his days in that school. Just before two in the morning the father, still furious, went off to bed. The mother gathered her scattered wits and wrote a letter so skilfully worded that even a teacher could not take exception to it.

But the letter caused no change in the boy's curriculum. Academically he wasted his primary years, emotionally he was so bottled up after school that his father, who worked at the Home Office, discussed with him the problems of frustration and juvenile delinquency. They begged him to withhold his anger until he got home. He would burst into the house, banging about angrily for a few minutes, and then some interesting hobby would catch his attention, so that he could settle happily. However, by mid-junior school they were glad to see that all his spare time was spent kicking a football with a friend. This was at least a step in social development. But he and his work presented such a scruffy appearance that they could not imagine that any grammar school would welcome him. So, contrary to their educational philosophy, they began to prepare him for the examination for a public school. They knew from the objective assessment made by a psychologist that only one in over 3,000 children would be as bright as their son, so there might be a chance that they could repair the damage. At the interview he was asked for his views on the Common Market, which Britain had not yet entered. There had been a talk at his school which, as happens with gifted children when they are interested, he seemed able to recall verbatim. In addition to this, he could argue two points of view about entering the Common Market as seen in two daily papers of somewhat differing standpoints. He was accepted, but, of course, he had never associated school with serious work so he came bottom of his form for a term or two. Then his attention was arrested and he rose to his rightful place, where he remained.

Some special abilities, such as musical talent, lend themselves to impressive display. Number prodigies can also astonish. Mathematicians, questioned about childhood interest in calculation, frequently tell of games played endlessly, such as walking home from school a new way to find a house the number of which is the square root of the number of their own house. They often evolve their own logarithmic tables before they know of printed ones, thus facilitating very complex unwritten calculations. One boy of nine went with his father to get a licence for something, and when he heard what number it was, burst out laughing. The number was 37542, which was just two less than the number of miles their old car had gone. His father said he was endlessly amusing himself in this way. As with music, there has to be a natural gift; but there also has to be continuous practice, whether it is called work or play. One serious problem with mathematical talent which has yet to be solved is that the most creative years for a brilliant mathematician are between approximately fifteen and twenty-one years. This period is passed before the child completes graduation, let alone is encouraged to do original postgraduate work. Thus, no matter what the gifts, the part played by home, school and university can be definitive, in positive or negative ways.

Let us compare two musical boys, one from a musical home and one from an equally cultured but unmusical home. The father of the first boy is himself a music master. His son expressed a great desire to play the violin when only four, but his father said he could not have lessons until he was six. However, when the boy was five he found an old violin in a cupboard, fitted it up with strings and taught himself to play. This broke down the father's resistance and lessons were started straight away. The other boy's parents, who claimed to be quite unmusical, were both in the legal profession. One evening, when they were washing up and their four-year-old son was playing with bricks on the kitchen floor, he suddenly burst into song, and what he sang was the first scene of *Don Giovanni*, in Italian. The parents were alarmed, and took him to a child guidance clinic where, on request, he repeated the performance. The psychologist thanked him and said that she had not been able to understand it all. With what might have been mistaken in earlier days for insolence, the four-year-old said he supposed not, as it was in Italian. When the parents were pressed for information about any musical ability anywhere in the family, the mother's own mother recalled a musical uncle who appeared to have squandered his ability; and the father proved able to whistle for him many melodies by specific composers of the war years some twenty-five years previously, such as those of Robert Farnon for the Black and White Minstrels. Apparently some felicitous coming together of genes from both sides of the family had resulted in startling musical ability. Under expert help, this boy was setting his own tunes to full orchestration by seven years of age. Once he had understood how the orchestration operated he needed no reference books while at work, a fact to impress most musicians. True, his tunes were only a few bars long but they were his own tunes that he orchestrated. It may be that this is the right order for a composer: first study the orchestration and then allow the themes to rise.

It is at times extremely difficult to distinguish when such gifts are due to heredity and when to environment. Certainly the talents have to be fostered. For example, one girl of some mathematical ability had two parents who were professors of mathematics, so it is fairly safe to assume that her ability was inherited. But the fact that both parents, when young, had loved to play mathematical games, meant that they now loved to re-play some of these games with their daughter, so that would be an environmental influence. It is safest to think of heredity and environment as two sides of a coin: both must be present or there is no coin. For social development, all children should learn to display their talents to the family and to friends, even if these 'performances' do not progress to public performances. But where, as in the case of music, public performance is desirable, much care has to be taken. The San Francisco Orchestra gave Yehudi Menuhin the opportunity for his debut when he was seven, and Isaac Stern his when he was eleven. In maturity the greatest artists – and the greatest scientists too – are notably modest. This is undoubtedly due to their awareness of the immensity of the art or science which they study.

The views of these children themselves are important. In March 1973 the *New York Times Magazine* published a long interview with the young violinist Lilit Gampel of Los Angeles. She had been billed as twelve when she was actually thirteen, which she rather resented, though she appreciated the publicity value of this. Beethoven had not realised that his father was billing him as two years younger than his actual age until he was adult. Asked what it was like to play for Heifetz, Lilit Gampel replied, 'Nice'. Asked what she thought of certain distinguished conductors with whom she had worked, she replied, 'What do you mean – Do I like them? You get to know them by playing for them, not talking.' Asked if she enjoyed discussions with the many great musicians she had met in her performances all over the world, she displayed her skilled technique for dodging unwelcome patronage by saying that she did not enjoy discussions with other musicians unless they had heard her play.

All the children described so far are real children. Their parents were physicists, lawyers, musicians, teachers, barristers, civil servants and so on. Though the causal effect of heredity and of environment is not easy to disentangle, we can note that all those concerned parents were middle class. They will have read about and pondered on the signs of exceptional ability, relating them to their own children. Yet we cannot conclude from this that gifts or talents are a middle-class phenomenon: Gauss, often acclaimed as the greatest mathematician of all time, was the son of a brick-layer; Laplace, almost as illustrious, was the son of a farm labourer; Marlowe and the father of John Stuart Mill were the sons of cobblers; James Watt and Carlyle were the sons of car-penters; Kant was the son of a strap-maker; Franklin the son of a soap-boiler; and Kepler the son of an innkeeper.

However, the fact that the so-called middle class is in a better position to become informed, to note the signs, and to foster ability, is born out by the following events. A group of middle-class parents got together in Kensington to discuss signs of giftedness in their children and their children's bad progress at school. They found it most helpful to share their problems, and particularly to meet some others who were experiencing the very same difficulties. In school their children were desperately bored and getting into mischief; at home they were sleeping much less than was normal for their age. They passed the time in bed reading at length on subjects about which they could not possibly have practical ex-perience, such as astronomy and physics, fossiliferous deposits and philosophy. Always there was the extraordinary experience of having to suppress discussion of the way their children behaved, if they or their children were to have any social life with the neigh-bours. They felt they should have an expert of some kind with whom to take over their difficulties but were not sure what kind of expert could help them best. One of them had heard of a social worker at a London teaching hospital, called Margaret Branch, and they invited her to come and meet them.

The outcome of that meeting was that Margaret Branch and her friend Camilla Ruegg, who had been an education lecturer, arranged a weekend conference in 1965, in Shropshire, under the chairmanship of Sir George Trevelyan. The participants were mainly mothers and a few fathers of gifted children. A small number of educationists attended, amongst whom were two educational psychologists, but in the main it was the parents who talked. Before the conference was over, those who thought that there should be an association designed to come to the rescue of these children paid fifty pence (ten shillings in those days) towards stationery and stamps. The organisation was informal and the subscription only a token one.

The following year, in 1966, the National Association for Gifted Children was formally registered.[1] Although the scholarship system has been running since 1893, just twenty-one years after the start of universal education in 1872, there were far more bright children in trouble than was realised, and for quite unsuspected reasons. During its first years the NAGC expanded at great speed and help was given to many thousands of bright children. Such a galaxy of distinguished people gave their support, that one had to suspect that their knowledge of the need for such an association was in many cases based on first-hand experience. When necessary, the Association can call upon the help of a panel of expert advisers whose experience is very wide. When Henry Collis retired from the headmastership of St Paul's Preparatory School, he took on the arduous task of becoming the Association's Director.

The reason why so much attention is given here to the National Association for Gifted Children is that it is the only body of its kind in the United Kingdom. Mensa, founded in 1945 following a broadcast by Professor Sir Cyril Burt, is formed on different lines for different purposes. The opportunity for membership of Mensa is attained by passing certain tests of intelligence intended to give objective evidence of an individual being in the intellectual top 2 per cent of the population; the purpose is to study problems and to offer suggestions for the benefit of all. There is a Young Mensa, but only for the sixteen to twenty age group. In contrast to this, the NAGC was set up in 1965 by a group of people deeply concerned that children of high ability were on the whole not receiving an education which permitted them normal development. The NAGC became an accredited charity the following year and its

[1] Those who wish to know more should write to Headquarters at 27 John Adam St, London WC2N 6HX.

chief work has been to analyse and rectify where possible the situation for the children.

The NAGC depends entirely upon donations, apart from a small Government grant and the annual £2 subscription (waived for poor families). Its members are welcomed for their interest and, modestly, few would claim to be in the highest echelons of intelligence themselves. However, the various activities run throughout many areas of Britain are specifically for children of high intellectual and artistic ability, together with such brothers and sisters as would like to join them. Parents are often referred to the Association by teachers, doctors, health visitors and nurses, who sometimes join the Association themselves. Teachers are less likely to refer them, because if the teachers are aware of the educational problems for outstandingly able children, they also know what adjustments can be made within the school. The Council of Management needs the advice of experts in different branches of the arts and sciences, concerning particular children. They invited various specialists, a mathematician, a musician, a physicist, an educational psychologists and so on to join a Panel of Advisers. The Panel is not a team, designed to work together, though on the rare occasions when as many as possible meet socially, they have a great deal to say to each other, and many matters can be raised for their consideration. But the valuable function that the Panel performs is this: individual specialists can be approached when advice is needed on individual children.

Branches cover much of the country and are run entirely by volunteers. They arrange out-of-school activities for the children, who are called 'Explorers Unlimited'. Brothers and sisters who may not be gifted are included for two reasons: first, it is not advisable to split families, and secondly, an important objective is to help gifted children to develop socially with those who may not be so gifted. Teachers, college of education and university lecturers and students help the parents in taking groups for such matters as astronomy, ecology, biology, drama, chess, pottery, painting, sculpture, music, photography, mathematical puzzles and computer programming. What activities are enjoyed depends partly on the questions the children ask, but also on what expertise happens to be available. Meeting other children as bright as themselves, or even brighter, also helps the 'Explorers' to become far more tolerant and tolerable. The NAGC also arranges summer courses offering subjects of special interest. Local education authorities who seek the help of the NAGC, and are willing to find teachers to help run Saturday workshops, use their own basis for selecting children.

Parents of gifted children enjoy meeting each other. They have problems in common which they can discuss. For instance, many gifted children require less sleep than is normal for children of their age. Frequently, after such discussions, a mother will say what a great relief it is to meet other mothers whose children need much less than average sleep, after thinking for years that there was something wrong in the way they managed their own children. Now that the NAGC has been responsible for so many programmes, published or broadcast, parents are themselves beginning to recognise such indications of ability as early eye focus, control of movement well in advance of average, signs of early reasoning (with or without speech) and the short sleep period. There is no one sign of intellectual gift or artistic talent; but a cluster of signs has meaning to the experts. Colleges of education are just beginning to include reference to exceptionally able children, though usually as one of the special areas of study, such as physical disability, mental subnormality etc. Those colleges which can encourage their students to regard the one or two exceptionally gifted or talented children who may emerge in any class as an exciting challenge are on the right lines. Such colleges sometimes invite groups of Explorers to work with their students, amongst the wonderful facilities of the college.

When students each take a child round to see what would be interesting to do, what is unquestionably of greatest moment to the gifted children is for each to have 'my student' as a private tutor attending to ceaseless questions, and taking a child to where he can find out answers for himself. Parents frequently invite the child's student home, which is invaluable for the student in having a glimpse of the child's background and a unique opportunity for the child to know the true meaning of returned hospitality. A notable proportion of parents of the NAGC have gone to very great lengths to act as universal tutor to their own children, with telescopes rigged up, microscopes in constant use, even a hired French horn. It is invaluable for students to see to what lengths such tutor-parents go, out of vivid companionship with the children. It is the task of the students' own tutors, when once more in college, to lead their thinking to how many gifted children are lost through being born into less fortunate families and at a time when the state is only just beginning to give support to solving the problems of gifted children at all levels, and in particular with families near the poverty line.

Some ideal of what it is like to work with such children can be seen in Bridges' (1969) *Gifted Children and the Brentwood Experiment*. This was not an NAGC experiment but it was one of the very first introductions on the special requirements of exceptionally able children, and it was one which won the co-operation of the local education authority, which is extremely important. Since that time, an increasing number of local education authorities are helping with activities such as the Saturday morning workshops. Many NAGC children have been to the Froebel Institute at Roehampton (Chapter 5 gives detailed accounts of a number of them, mostly members of the Surrey Branch). More and more students, in training for teaching, are choosing this area for special study, which is a first step towards postgraduate work in the field of able children. The early pioneering stage of the NAGC was over in 1973. That year the Department of Education and Science gave the NAGC its official support and ran its first open course in the teaching of gifted children in primary and middle school, inviting the Director and General Secretary of the NAGC to be on the staff of the course.

Naturally, parents would like a checklist of signs of high ability to work their way through, so that they could decide for themselves whether they had such a child. There are, however, two reasons why this does not seem to be the best approach for them. First, a list can be given but only someone who has made a deep study of child psychology, and specifically of the psychology of children notably above average, can decide which parameters are most likely to suggest high ability. As soon as you get a coming-together of abilities, the matter becomes one of intuitive assessment of relationships, and here the expert is more reliable than the amateur. The State does not yet even stipulate that couples who intend to have children make a study, according to their ability, of what rearing a normal child is like. When they do, there will be fewer 'unmanageable' children because more parents, at all levels of society, will know how to avoid creating unnecessary difficulties for their children. We cannot expect parents who have not made a study of normal children to recognise a supernormal child. Only when all parents expect to have some simple course on child psychology can they become allies of professional psychologists in detecting these especially able children. Secondly, some of the supposedly most reliable signs, like alertness and short hours of sleep, can be quite misleading. For instance, G. K. Chesterton seemed in his schooldays a stodgy and sleepy boy; his masters thought he was usually asleep, and he said they were usually right. If parents suspect that they have a supernormal child, they can either get in touch with the NAGC, saying why they think so, or themselves seek objective assessment. In the latter case, for artistic talents, they have to consult a specialist in the art, and for intellectual gifts they should consult an educational psychologist.

One would expect the school to inform the parents on these matters, but there is an important reason why not. The school is under the local education authority, and not free to offer such reports to parents. The child guidance clinics are also under LEAs, and though they have educational psychologists, they also are not free to offer parents their reports. Moreover, the clinics are run for children who are emotionally upset in some way, and gifted children are as balanced as other children unless mishandled. But child guidance clinics are to be found in every county, and they will always tell you how to have your child assessed by an educational psychologist, and may have someone on the clinic staff who is in private practice as well. Such a person is free to make a general assessment and pass on the findings to the parent who pays the fee. The reason why assessment of intelligence is such a skilled task is explained in Chapter 3, while in Chapter 4 the special problems of assessing talent in the various arts are discussed. Whether parents decide to approach the NAGC first or to approach an educationally qualified psychologist privately, what matters is that the right steps are taken to obtain an objective assessment.

There has been a strong element of inertia in our unwillingness to face the idea that our supernormal children might be in trouble. The argument runs as follows: we have universal education adapted for the ablest children through examinations and scholarships; the authorities tend to think that the children cannot be very able if they cannot find their own way through such help. What has gone wrong is to be found in the fact that many able children fit very badly into the regimentation of school life. Many have independent and divergent opinions. They see the flaws in the teachers' arguments and the gaps in their knowledge; their own ideas may be not only different but also much better. The harassed teacher, struggling to help the rest of the class, may give a very poor showing in brusquely forbidding the brightest to interrupt any more. It was because they had so often been told not to talk in school, that the children so enjoyed having students as private tutors when visiting the colleges of education. Parents of educationally subnormal children saw much sooner that their children needed special adaptation of the curriculum, and by now some of these children actually have schools designed especially for them. Whether the supernormal children need as much done for them is discussed in the final chapter. But something has to be done, along the lines of the pioneering NAGC activities, and eventually parents of the ablest children will also have to rouse sufficient support from many quarters for government action to become inevitable.

In the process of breaking through this barrier of inertia, we shall come across many anomalies in our educational system which we must examine closely if we are to be able to make the necessary changes. Why, for example, do we speak of infants' schools, when they are for children who are far past infancy? Why do we speak of public schools when those who go there know very well that they are private schools? Historically, we can see how they got their names. The children were called infants because everyone had thought them too young to educate; but the philanthropists wanted to get the five-year-olds out of the factories and mines, and so it is that we have an earlier start of school than almost any other country in the world. With the start of universal education more than a century ago, teachers soon saw what the factory-owners had long seen: these children were teachable and could learn fast. Some schools are called public schools because they are a remnant of an old and honourable school system which really was public.

Why were only the boys educated? It is necessary to go very far back in time to find that out. The Romans, who started the first schools here, were held up in their plans by a woman, Boudicca, Queen of the Iceni in Norfolk and Suffolk. Could this partly explain some eighteen centuries of not educating any girls? Today, we are having to think so fast to save the world that we cannot allow old prejudices to hold us up any longer. In the second half of the nineteenth century the inequality of the sexes began to be questioned. The evolution of events goes so fast that this inequality of the sexes may almost disappear by the end of the twentieth century. That is a great acceleration: for eighteen centuries women were repressed and in two centuries or less they are gaining their rightful place. We cannot ignore such questions because they are highly relevant. Are gifted children a modern phenomenon? Indeed not. Only the gifted boys were selected until universal education came in 1872. Would it be better to go back to having special education for the supernormal children? We have a special education for the subnormal children, with most exciting results. We ought to think of our need for the most developed and the wisest to steer the world through coming events, both near and far in time. Does this mean special schools for the most exceptionally gifted? Comprehensive schools might have to be thought of as having neither the bottom nor the top two or three per cent of children, in terms of ability and aptitude. Answers to some of these questions are sought in the next chapter. But the crying need is for more high-level research on supernormal children.

2

GIFTED CHILDREN THROUGH THE CENTURIES

In a Foreword to *Able Misfits* by Kellmer Pringle (1970), Professor Sir Cyril Burt[1] began with an important quotation on the occasion of the introduction of the London County Council's scholarship scheme. 'Britain,' said Sir Robert Blair, 'was the first nation to recognise the importance of making special provision for the education of her ablest children; it must be our aim to do this regardless of distinction of wealth, influence, or social class.' That was in 1893, eleven years after the commencement of education for all children, girls as well as boys, poor as well as rich, average and dull as well as bright. The revolution was not in making State education free – for many centuries able boys had been educated free, and in any case, the State had to make it free to avoid some parents objecting that they had not the money to afford the luxury of education. The real revolution was twofold: including girls as well as boys, and educating children of all levels of ability. Burt, going briefly into the historical background of care for able boys, shows how the gifted received the special care of education, but in the struggle for universal education the brightest children had been pushed aside until the start of the scholarships, and even then many of the brightest were failing. He concludes his Foreword by saying of Dr Pringle's criticism of the present situation for gifted children, that he is in whole-hearted agreement with her dissatisfaction.

Going back still further than Burt takes us to even deeper roots of our educational system. For nearly two thousand years in these islands only very bright boys were accepted for education. More

---

[1] Professor Sir Cyril Burt, MA, DSc, DLitt, FBA, was the first psychologist to be appointed to an education authority in the UK. The London County Council appointed him in 1913 and his first task was to report on backward children.

than half these centuries were before the invention of printing, so there are few direct indications of how these boys were first taught. We know that the selection technique was one with which we are very familiar today: the boys had to demonstrate that they had learned to read. When the Romans conquered Britain, the alphabet was already between one and two thousand years old. Diringer (1962), in his book called *Writing*, estimates from a considerable accumulation of evidence, that the system of writing which we call alphabetic was invented in the Middle East fairly early in the second millennium BC. He thinks the concept of representing the various sounds in words separately originated with one master mind. But as it covered all known languages around the whole Mediterranean area at that time, the final reduction of all the sounds to an elegant code involving the minimum of letters must have been the work of a team of able men, once the brilliant concept had been invented. The process of decoding which we call reading, and which we expect of children at a very early age, is immensely more complex than has been suspected until quite recent times. The child has to recognise and, when he fails to recognise, try a whole system of probable answers which may have to be thrown aside as not leading to comprehension.

The alphabet has been taught to children for three to four thousand years, always with a high proportion of failures. That is to say, some children were so good that they seemed to teach themselves; a much higher proportion could eventually read but would not; and some could never understand what it was about. The National Committee for Adult Literacy, of which Lady Plowden is the President, aims to achieve universal literacy; and my personal experience is that the illiterate adults know the alphabet perfectly well, but have no idea what to do with it. It is worth our while just touching on the new way of helping children to read. We have applied the alphabet to children and expected them to ply it back as nearly untouched as possible. But children are not passive. They are active, planning, decision-making people, working on their own data-processing activities. What they want is not just information but evidence. For example, *cat* is a short alphabetic word marked on the page with black ink; but it is also a sweet, furry thing that can get up, stretch and say 'Miaow'. We have to use every known way of getting the alphabetic word across: look-and-say, alphabet, writing, repetition, saying the alphabet, spelling out the word, anything to make learning that part fun. But such ingenious ways are only the means; the ends are to get that word into the realms of thought, so that the child wants to know what happened to the cat. This is indeed a revolution in teaching reading. Anyone who wishes to go further into modern work on reading should take the Open University Reading Development course, which can be one unit towards a degree.

The whole history of the alphabet is curiously chequered and blocked. Logically it should have spread abroad quickly, wherever the intelligent merchants plied their trade, but it did not. There is a possibility that it reached Ireland through the Phoenician merchants travelling along the Atlantic coasts of Portugal, Spain and France. But if so, it was kept a priestly secret, as there was already in Ireland a method of recording events. It is worth noting that tree-worship existed at that time, and that the Irish alphabet today has letters named after trees, as one might say Ash, Birch, Chestnut, etc.

The greater part of the period under review is history common to the new and the old world. Before the Pilgrim Fathers left for America in 1620 they lived in Europe and their forbears were our forbears. If we go back to the Romans in Gaul, this is mutual history for the Americans and Europe; and going back to the Romans in Britain, this is mutual history for us and the United States until long after the Declaration of Independence in 1776. Caesar failed to conquer the British Isles in 55 and 54 BC. The Romanisation of these isles began with Claudius in AD 43. It was to last between three and four centuries. One cannot be more precise than that, because Roman organisation was so good that it continued for a while after the legions were recalled to Rome. During their first forty years the Romans built an impressive network of roads throughout England, Wales and southern Scotland. They planned to complete it in thirty years, but met strenuous opposition in East Anglia from the Iceni, led by Queen Boudicca.

The precise significance of Queen Boudicca's opposition becomes clear when one recalls that the Greeks, from whom the Roman culture originated, had suffered a long battle with the

Southern matriarchy centred in Crete. The Greeks had to over-suppress their women, and now for a whole decade the Romans were unable to be certain that they could suppress the women in these islands. The Romans won, and naturally thought it best to over-suppress the women here too. That there was a matriarchal system, with a queen to lead the most resistant area, shows clearly that the concept of suppressing women was not indigenous to these islands, but brought by the Romans. Robert Graves, in *The White Goddess*, describes the matriarchal system in Britain before the Romans came. We shall see in Chapter 4 that we ignore the insights of our poets at our peril.

The Romans selected their schoolboys according to whether they had learned to read alphabetically by seven or eight. Modern research shows that it is round about mental age seven or eight that the principle upon which the alphabet is based begins to be grasped. Before that mental age, children use a whole complex system of ingenious ideas to help them jump to what a word means. We also know that, on the whole, boys are slower to read than girls; and some very able children, particularly boys, reason by calculation rather than words, so that reading alone is not a good method of discovering non-verbal ability of these children. Nor is poor vision an indication of stupidity. We are much nearer to these now-exploded theories than we realise. Professor Burt's father, a country doctor, was sure Christ's Hospital was mistaken in using sight as a test of ability. So, knowing that his son was shortsighted, he taught him all the letters on the vision chart before he went for his interview. 'Otherwise,' said the Professor, 'it might not have been this professor that you met at this college.'

The schools started by the Romans were of their customary kind. There were no school buildings. Tutors would gather the ablest boys they could find, and work with them in any available free space. We know they charged a fee and that the fee was not always easy to get, because Lucian (AD 117–80) wrote a satire on the problem of obtaining the fees. A number of schools still in existence have a legend that they were founded where old Roman schools were sited. They are all situated on junctions of important Roman roads, and the legends may well be true. The relevance of the road junctions is that travelling men of ability might very likely be glad to pause and earn a little money where there was no one to teach the boys. The boys had to learn to calculate, for civil engineering and for commerce. They also studied rhetoric, for argument on legal and governmental matters, and for handing on as oral tradition. These able boys had to learn to speak well, both by rote and spontaneously; and of course they would have to write, and to read classical literature.

From the Roman viewpoint, the conquest of these islands was no more than an extension of Gaul. Movement over the whole area was free, rather as envisaged by the Common Market idea today. Pottery and other crafts were adult occupations. The boys would see mosaic experts arriving with a packet of designs, for clients to select the design they wanted just as wallpaper can be selected from books today. The mosaics were so well laid that some of them can still be seen today. We may be sure that schoolboys watched the laying of mosaics and the building in progress before they were old enough to leave school and become civil engineers or craftsmen themselves. In school a fine level of classical Latin was used; but outside, where all the constructional work was in progress, a vulgar Latin of the people was spoken.

Where large groups of boys gathered for education, the schoolmaster had an usher or doorkeeper, to see that the boys joined their tutor in a seemly way. In the crook of his arm the usher held an upturned birch. This would have been more as a reminder of good behaviour than for practical application. All over Gaul this remnant of tree worship (the birch was one of the sacred trees as well as a handy shape for thrashing) was carried as a symbol of seemly conduct on ceremonial occasions, such as purchase of property, when birch was used to 'beat the bounds'. But these schoolmasters had to get their fees from their pupils; so they are not likely to have jeopardised rapport with the boys by literally applying the birch themselves.

When the barbarians from the east were beating upon the gates of Rome in AD 410, the legions, groups of about forty thousand soldiers, had to be recalled to Rome. But a reasonably stable organisation had been established in the British Isles. So the message came from Rome, that non-soldiers left behind should fend for themselves as best they could. This they did. Until the late 1960s it was assumed that the level of living classical Latin declined sharply, once the legions had left. Gildas, writing around AD 530 and used today for references to the early Christian faith here, was supposed to be a clerk of indifferent literary ability. Then in 1968 Kerlouégan produced a very closely reasoned article, explaining that repeated poor-quality translations over the centuries had completely obscured the style of Gildas. Kerlouégan concludes from the original writings that Gildas wrote a highly cultured Latin, quite out of the mainstream of European Latin. He says it suggests a continuing tradition of pedantic school-masterly Latin in Britain, though in somewhat of a backwater after the breakdown of Roman authority. At the time that Gildas was writing, barbarians from the east had poured into these islands. Yet even under these circumstances, more than a century after the Roman legions had left, there was a high level of classical Latin written, and presumably written for others to read.

It is asking a great deal that we should believe the Roman influence still to be with us today, or at least until the 1872 introduction of universal education. Yet the system did remain entirely patriarchal with only boys educated in schools for some eighteen centuries; and women are still, in the late twentieth century, fighting for equality of opportunity. Moreover, since only the ablest boys went to school, no one can claim that the special treatment of gifted children is a modern phenomenon.

Right up to the introduction of education for all, irrespective of ability and sex, selection of gifted children has been by alphabetic reading. We know now that this selection technique is likely to miss non-verbal children of ability. But we are not entirely free of those who give the alphabet top priority, instead of using a wide variety of techniques and leaving the child to jump to the principle of the alphabet as and when he is ready. Nor are we free of those who advocate application of the birch, which is a degradation of the symbolic way in which the Romans used the birch as a reminder of law and order. The term 'usher' also stayed in many schools throughout the centuries, though State schools now expect the teachers to be their own ushers; and the birch is in many a head's cupboard as a concealed threat. We cannot claim that good tutorial discussions on current affairs, modern literature, ethical conduct, and so on, are inventions of twentieth-century progressive schools, because that kind of discussion was of the essence of Roman education. It was only in later ages that stereotyped teaching of a dead language replaced living Latin. The claim, therefore, that Roman schooling has had a profound influence upon our educational system is not without foundation.

Exactly when St Augustine reached these islands is not known. The Christian faith seems to have come ahead of him, as there are early Roman mosaics which include Christian symbols such as the cross and the fish. But we do know that he opened Canterbury Cathedral in AD 598, upon the site of an old temple. He needed men for the offices of the church and boys for the choir. So, a few years later, very early in the seventh century, he opened a choir school, called King's, Canterbury, which is still in existence today. It has a legend that it was built on the site of one of the Roman schools, and there were certainly important roads leading to and from Canterbury, with considerable traffic for those days. Nobody has yet questioned this school's claim to be the oldest school in Britain, and the first with purpose-built premises. The language of education was Ecclesiastical Latin, as for many centuries it was with all succeeding choir schools. The choir schools which exist today and which claim to be founded on the sites of Roman schools include in addition to Canterbury those at York, Bristol, Ely, St Albans and Wells. These are all areas rich in Roman remains which are visited every year by very many people. Apart from the rituals for the church, we have little evidence of what education went on. Consequently it is worth noting of the choir boys' recreation an old document at Ely, dating halfway back to the beginning of choir schools, which states that, on wet days, the boys could trundle their hoops and spin their tops in the aisles of the cathedral.

The Middle Ages can be taken as stretching three or four hundred years either side of the year 1000. This covered some eight hundred years, during which all culture was dedicated to the glory of God and individual people are almost never mentioned. However, in the second half of the eighth century a brilliant man wrote a remarkable account of his own headmaster at St Peter's, York. The writer was Alcuin (AD 735–804). As a source, he seems impeccable. He was called to Aix by Charlemagne to help in educational reform there, and later became Abbot of Tours. Of his St Peter's headmaster, Alcuin wrote: 'To some he diligently gave the art of the use of grammar, pouring into others the streams of rhetoric. These he polished on the grindstone of the law, those he taught to sing Aeonian chant,[1] . . . others the aforesaid master caused to know the harmony of the sky . . . the tides and earth-quakes . . . and especially did he unveil the mysteries of Holy Scripture. . . . Whatever youths he saw of remarkable intelligence, he got hold of them, taught them, fed them, cherished them.'

Alcuin gives evidence of the birch now literally being used on the boys. He refers to 'necessary' birchings, 'that they should grow to man's estate with whippings of fatherly discipline and [become] strong with learning of sacred rules'. It is interesting to note that in the latter part of the Middle Ages, in 1350, the birch as a symbol was brought back into Parliament, as unruly a place at times as any schoolroom. From that year onwards, at the opening and closing of every day of Parliament, the Gentleman Usher Official of the House of Lords leads a procession; and in the crook of his arm is the black rod, that members be reminded to deport themselves as gentlemen. It is a small but very impressive little twice-daily procession which bears the important message, with symbolic birch and watchful usher of Roman times.

This was about the time that the Anglo-Norman kings were withdrawing to these islands from the battles still raging in Europe. The Normans were beginning to appreciate the relatively settled conditions away from the stormy continent, and a large court developed in London. There was a shortage of lawyers, clerks, justices and other personnel for the running of this elaborate bureaucracy. In order to staff the court, the Anglo-Norman noble-men were forced to look outside their ranks. That any positions of authority should pass from the hands of the nobility was contrary to the feudal system and this decision may well have been the initial cause of the collapse of feudalism. Feudal law depended upon the first-born for administration of the land, with noblemen inheriting the great estates and franklins inheriting tools for their

---

[1] This quotation is from Gardner (1973), p. 11. Aeonian chants may have been based upon Platonic philosophical notions of a power existing from eternity in emanation from the supreme deity.

strips of land. The courts were run for the noblemen, and it was they who needed administrators. The clergy were celibate, so had no descendants. The practical merchants turned to the younger sons of noblemen. But there were not enough of them, so they looked about for bright boys of any class, and began to educate them for secular office. In the years between the Norman Conquest and Henry VIII's Dissolution of the Monasteries, more than three hundred grammar schools were opened all over the country. Amongst them were four, still in existence today: Norwich, founded in 1250, Abingdon in 1256, Bablake in 1344 and Durham in 1414.

With only carefully selected, gifted boys chosen to train for court administration, the court prospered even more rapidly. A new source of human energy in the community had been tapped and the feudal lords, while despising the clerkly underlings, did not see them as any kind of threat to the established feudal hierarchy. But not only did the professional class grow, a powerful merchant class also emerged, and began to amass private fortunes without claiming to be noblemen. When there were no offspring to inherit, they began to wonder what to do with this wealth. Soon some of the merchant fortunes began even to surpass the wealth of the Church. Moreover, this wealth had not been stolen from the Church, as some merchants felt the Church was stealing their money. It was, they felt, the property of those who had earned it: the corn-millers, brewers, coopers, mercers, bell-founders and all the other traders. There are two threads in man's disposition: egotism, which ensures survival of the individual, and altruism, which ensures survival of future generations. Rich merchants with children of their own supported laws of inheritance which safeguarded their children. But many rich merchants were childless and some of these had been poor bright boys, even foundlings, who had worked their way up, either losing touch with their families not even knowing if they had relatives. A number of these childless merchants left wills with altruistic instructions for the foundation of schools for poor but able boys, often in association with almshouses for the old.

These new merchant schools were the first secular schools since Roman times. It is hard for us today to understand the independ-

ence of thought required to break away and found secular
grammar schools. But that is not the only strain upon our imagina-
tions. Today, after over a century of studying how best to teach,
we naturally assume that a different kind of school for a different
purpose would require a different syllabus. But there were no
educational committees or panels or commissions. For a thousand
years the purpose for which the brightest boys had been selected
had been religious practice. The merchants, unable to imagine
what could be taught besides Latin and Religious Instruction,
which had been all the education that anyone they knew had
received, left these two subjects as virtually the entire curriculum.
There was one adjustment which they made that somehow under-
lines their humble ignorance of how children should be educated.
Since the Norman Conquest, all schools had used Norman French
for teaching. The merchant schools changed the language of
teaching to English. But they entirely missed the point that they
had removed the purpose in teaching Latin and Religious Instruction. Latin as a living language gradually died away; and religion,
taught for no high purpose, also proved unsatisfactory for intelligent boys. Boys and schoolmasters alike became deeply bored,
one of the major disasters for able people, young or old. The
merchant schools, so enterprisingly embarked upon, began to
wither away, and nobody could understand why.

This state of deterioration in schools puzzled the merchants.
They wondered whether their independence of the Church had
offended God; or whether as much care had been given to selecting teachers as to selecting pupils. Eventually they planned a
school which would overcome every possible error they might
have inadvertently committed. As building entrepreneur they
chose a man so brilliant that he went on to help build Windsor
Castle, then became the first Bishop of Winchester, and was finally
made Lord Chancellor. This was William of Wykeham and the
school was Winchester College, founded in 1382 and opened
twelve years later. The beautiful school chapel was a great wonder
and many visitors came to see it, including royalty. The foundation
consisted of a warden, ten fellows, three lay clerks, seventy poor
and needy scholars, and sixteen choristers for the beautiful school
chapel. Wykeham realised that one of the worst deficiencies of the

secular schools was that they were attached to no great established institution, and so lacked incentive for the brighter boys to attain places there. He showed his great vision in first opening a university where the brighest boys could continue their studies. This was New College, Oxford, founded for 'an hundred poor clerks'. To this day the brightest Winchester boys tend to go on to New College, Oxford.

In 1418 Sevenoaks School in Kent was founded by Sir William Sevenoke. He is said to have been a foundling discovered in the streets and, as was customary, was given the name of the town where he was found. He became an honoured London grocer, being made Alderman of the Tower Ward and Warden of the Grocer's Company, Mayor of the City; and eventually he was knighted. He was a well-known philanthropist and to celebrate Agincourt made foundations for a school and almshouses at Sevenoaks. His concern for the community remains a tradition with the school and today extends to international understanding. There are exchanges with schools in Paris, including a common Anglo-French form with a French school, and an 'international centre' for sixth-formers in which two-thirds of the boys are from overseas. A voluntary service run jointly with local State schools involves the boys in the problems of the elderly, of young people in trouble, and also the physically and mentally handicapped. This continuity – and development – of tradition puts Sevenoaks School in the vanguard of what are now called public schools.

The next school to be founded was to become the most famous school in Europe, perhaps in the world. This is, of course, Eton. Henry VI decided to have an even finer school than Winchester, and to have it on his own doorstep. The building was under the supervision of Waynflete, almost as remarkable a man as Wykeham. The King named it 'The King's General School' and called it the lady, mother and mistress of all other grammar schools. But it was always known by where it was built. For its maintenance he gave the school certain valuable London properties, including what is now Leicester Square, Piccadilly and part of Mayfair. The original foundation was laid in 1441. It was to have a provost, ten priests, four clerks, six choristers, a schoolmaster, twenty-five poor and needy scholars and twenty-five poor men. Following

Wykeham's idea, Henry VI opened in the same year, 1441, King's College, Cambridge, to take scholars from Eton. Provision was also made for fee-paying sons of rich and noble parents. It was in this last direction that Eton was compelled to develop when Henry VIII, caring nothing for education but much for property, took away the London areas left by Henry VI for maintenance. The school has always been divided into two sections: collegers, who are the scholars; and oppidans, who are fee-paying. The life of collegers was always, by most accounts, quite hideous; but the oppidans were in reasonable comfort, with dames to see to their needs and private tutors to see to their education. Eton became a school for the royal, noble and wealthy. In the main, only the collegers are relevant to the theme of this book.

Waynflete was determined to have both a college and a school of his own, and close together, like King's, Canterbury and the cathedral it served. In 1448 he founded Magdalen College, Oxford; it opened in 1480. Beside it he founded Magdalen College School, where boys could be grounded in Latin before entering the college proper. The invention of printing was at that time still very new. The grammarians of the school set down in print their methods of teaching Latin. This information could now spread quickly and masters of other schools, many of them famous, were instructed to use these methods. Looking back from today, it is interesting to note that the manuals were for masters, not for boys. They continued teaching Latin as it always had been taught – orally.

When Henry VIII (1491–1547) came to the throne, he found a much quicker way of making money than the hard-working merchants. He stole it from the Church by dissolving the very rich monasteries; and he stole it from the rich merchants by closing more than three hundred of their grammar schools and taking the endowments for himself. A handful of schools escaped closure for one reason or another: they were too poor and unimportant, or, as with St Paul's in the City of London, surrounded by powerful merchants with whom the king did not dare risk too much conflict. He did not actually close Winchester or Eton. These two schools had been the pride of kings. But he took away their money; and he took from Eton the valuable London Mayfair property, which had been left to them for running expenses by their farsighted founder. Thus Eton was virtually compelled to take as fee-paying boys the sons of wealthy courtiers visiting royalty at Windsor. These aristocrats had been arguing for some time that, if poor boys could be educated free, rich boys should be allowed to be educated for fees. The oppidans, the rich boys, lived in relative comfort. The collegers, the poor but able scholars, had by most accounts a horrific time. Their numbers dwindled; they lived and slept in one room; and masters rarely dared to visit them.

Henry VIII had little care for the future. He could have argued that his burning desire for an heir was indication of his concern for the future. But it was care for his own future, not for the future of all his people's children. His instability is shown by his muddled thinking. Without losing his faith, he stole from the Church and he insisted on divorces, which his Church did not allow. He imagined that a divorce granted in such a way must legitimise an heir. The only one of his divorces which concerns us here is the first. He married his father's widow, and when he wanted to get rid of her, remembered that his first marriage had been incestuous. Elizabeth was born into a chaotic household, the traumatic experiences from which were to affect her all her life. Elizabeth was brilliant. No new approaches to history question this. Her mother, Anne Boleyn, came from the rising merchant class, the poor but able boys who had been educated. Anne Boleyn's father was a financial genius, but he persistently and skilfully refused to take high office until he was knighted. As Sir William Boleyn he accepted the post of Keeper of the Exchange at Calais and the Foreign Exchange in London. His daughter, Anne Boleyn, was equally skilful. She would not consider a close relation with Henry VIII without the sanction of wedlock. This was the cause of the first divorce, and also the cause of Elizabeth's birth being 'legitimate'. But the court despised the Boleyns. Why?

The court knew of their humble origins. Philologists today will recognise the link between Boleyn and Villein. A bestowed knighthood could not, in a feudal society, change Sir William Boleyn into an aristocrat. One had to be born into the aristocracy. Then, as now, amassing a fortune had to be several generations back for the robbery stage to be overlooked. The court knew that the grandfather of Sir William Boleyn had been a serf, the lowest rung of the feudal system. The meteoric rise of the Boleyns which the noblemen could not tolerate was this: Anne Boleyn had risen from serf to wife of a king in only four generations, and Elizabeth herself had risen from serf to queen in her own right in only five generations. In the Foreword mentioned above, Burt (1970) suggests that the intellectual brilliance of Elizabeth I came, not as commonly supposed from the Tudors, but from the Boleyns.

This sheds a different light upon Elizabeth's reign. Modern research now shows that exceptionally brilliant children who are not given a chance to converse with their intellectual equals become totally discouraged about communicating with those around them. Most of the courtiers, unlike the Boleyns and other merchants, were virtually without education. Moreover, a greater difference is now found between the intellectual level of a brilliant child and an average grammar school child than between an average grammar school child and a child now assessed as mentally subnormal. In addition to this intellectual isolation, there was the social climate of contempt for her maternal origins, of ridicule for the notion that girls might be educated, and the traumatic experience of having her mother beheaded on what was probably a trumped-up charge of adultery. Elizabeth's tutors said she devoured knowledge; but as a woman she was not supposed to do so. She grew into a queen who, from personal experience, despised the stupidity and dishonesty and flattery of the court. She trusted no one there and, from what she had seen of court intrigues and her own father's succession of marriages, she decided that she herself would never marry. But this was the court which surrounded her and with which she had to work. She manipulated them with complex manoeuvres so far beyond their comprehension that they had to have recourse to 'female illogicality' as the only possible explanation of her behaviour.

The powerful and wealthy merchants had been deeply distressed by the loss of their prized schools. With a little pressure, they persuaded the reluctant Henry VIII to open a few schools, even to re-endow some grammar schools. When Edward VI came to the throne, he took a keen interest in education, and re-opened many more schools. It has generally been assumed that when

Elizabeth came to the throne she was not interested in education and the merchants merely flattered her by suggesting that when charters were granted for schools they should be specifically named Elizabethan Grammar Schools. This brilliant woman must have known even better than the contemptuous nobility how the educated Boleyns had risen in society. The courtiers would not know why the Boleyns had risen, because they did not value education. She probably took a keen interest in her step-brother's efforts to re-establish education for poor but able boys in his short reign. But after her father had built a navy with the finances from the Church and the schools, she was extremely short of money. Even so, she managed to re-open more old schools, and she even founded new ones. The tradition that she was not interested in education probably arose from two sources: first, as a woman, no one at court would expect her to be interested in education, and then, as a brilliant but very isolated monarch, she could rarely explain to those around her what her long-terms plans were. She never complained of the flattery of merchants, only of courtiers.

By degrees, royal permission was granted to open once more the choir and grammar schools, now completely separated from the Catholic Church. From time to time a new school would be started, for instance Westminster School, in the Dean's Yard, the Abbey now being Protestant. One of the most remarkable schools never to have closed was St Paul's, in the heart of the City of London. What had been a modest Church grammar school was transformed into a major institution of the Worshipful Company of Mercers. John Colet, who founded the school, was the son of a prosperous mercer. He became a priest and then, in 1504, Dean of St Paul's Cathedral. When his father died he left his son a small fortune. Six years later John Colet opened this merchant-endowed school of St Paul's right in the City of London, the very heart of commerce. There were to be 153 scholars, all free. They were to be in the care of three well-chosen men, a highmaster, an undermaster and a chaplain. According to Gardner (1973), Colet put his plans in writing: 'In this scole shall be first an Hyghe Maister. This Hyghe Maister, in doctrine, in learnynge and teachynge, shall direct the scole . . . a man hoole in body, honest and vertuous, and learned in good cleane Laten Literature, and also Greke, yf such may be gotten.' He also stated that there should be 'children of all nations and contres indifferently', provided each boy could 'saye the Catechyzon, and also he can rede and write'. We can see how such idealism within a realistic merchant tradition could completely bypass religious intolerance, with single-minded purpose to educate future generations in the best known way. Incidentally it was because our society stabilised so early that our spelling was and still is, so erratic. When other countries became literate, most could profit by seeing that spelling should be rationalised. Martin Luther (1483–1546) was nearly halfway through translating the Bible when he saw how to systematise German spelling, and began again. We also see now, but inertia prevents the change.

Five of the old merchant-founded grammar schools which survived the dissolution of the monasteries, or were re-founded, retained the old term 'grammar' and are still in existence today. These are : Royal (1469), Stockport (1487), Queen Elizabeth's, Blackburn (1509), Wolverhampton (1512) and Manchester (1515). Manchester Grammar School, for a long time financed by the profits from local corn mills, has had a very distinguished career. One school which may have a very ancient history, but only claims certain existence from 1552, is Shrewsbury. The course of events here was typical of what was happening. The townspeople of Shrewsbury were worried by their lack of educational facilities after the religious change. So they petitioned Henry VIII for a grammar school. Permission was granted in 1552, which means that petitioning for the opening of schools must have begun almost before Henry VIII had finished closing the monasteries and schools, as it took years to persuade the king to open a school again. How much this school was needed can be seen from the fact that within thirty years Shrewsbury was the largest school in England. Merchant Taylors' School took a title highlighting the source of its funds when founded in 1506. It was linked to St John's College, Oxford. One school, Rugby, was founded in 1567, but did not become famous until the coming of Dr Thomas Arnold in 1828.

Between the slow re-opening of schools in the latter part of the sixteenth century and the arrival of Dr Arnold at Rugby early in the nineteenth century, the schools sank to such a low ebb, both here and all over Europe, that very little reference is made to education through these years. This was a decadent period in social history. It is known to most people through Hogarth's series of pictures which he called *The Rake's Progress*. William Hogarth (1697–1764) regarded himself as a dramatist, although his pictures were still. For instance, in the picture of this series which he called 'The Orgy', there are countless clues that a dozen people are on the verge of shifting from frenzied excitement to drunken stupor and only two are withdrawn spectators. The Pilgrim Fathers fled from Delft and Plymouth to the New World across the Atlantic in 1620. They were rigidly convinced that America was intended for them by God, and they remained so convinced, even though they had first to exterminate most of the Red Indians and then to exterminate most of the Spanish Catholics on the Californian coast. Nevertheless, the old continent suffered from the departure of those rigid idealists. Idealism sank even lower.

Education is inherently idealistic, because it is designed for adults of the future. The number of people in the community who could think in such terms declined rapidly, and this had a disastrous effect upon the schools. The lowest ebb of education occurred during the seventeenth and early eighteenth centuries. Table 1 shows the disastrous loss of endowed schools during this period. The graph is based on the number of endowed schools which had survived or were reformed under the erroneous title of 'public schools' by 1973. Grasping men, even university academics, cast covetous eyes upon the endowments, as Henry VIII had done before them. Under these circumstances, discipline was attempted by horrifying use of the birch. None of the great schools seem to have avoided reputations for cruelty; and many schools closed because only a handful of pupils were sent there. Gardner (1973), writes, for instance, 'By the nineteenth century Merchant Taylors' was, like so many great schools, struggling in the decayed shell of former respectability. Conditions were almost as bad as those at Westminster,' and so on. One master was an invalid and ordered gentle exercise by his doctor, so he systematically flogged the boys while sitting down, till they were, according to one old boy, 'striped with dark streaks like a zebra'.

Table 1   GRAPH OF FOUNDATION DATES OF THE 218 PUBLIC SCHOOLS
OF 1973

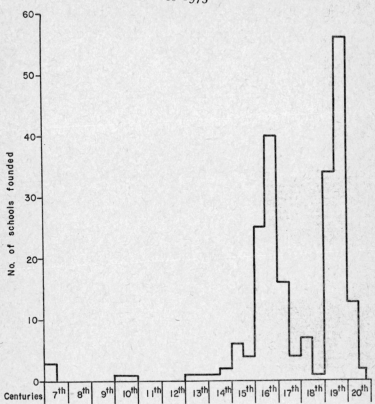

Table 1   GRAPH OF FOUNDATION DATES OF THE 218 PUBLIC SCHOOLS OF 1973

1   Sixteenth-century reigns: Henry VIII   1509–47
    Edward VI   1547–53
    Mary Tudor   1553–58
    Elizabeth I   1558–1603

2   Before Henry VIII's reign the merchants had endowed more than 300 secular schools. Henry VIII closed almost all of them, but was then compelled to open a score or so.

3   Edward was interested in education but only lived three years into the second half of the sixteenth century. Three of the King Edward schools were founded the year before he died. This leaves more than

a dozen endowed secular schools founded by Elizabeth, despite her financial troubles.

4   The Pilgrim Fathers left in 1620, very soon after the death of Elizabeth, because of the decline in moral standards.

5   For two centuries after the death of Elizabeth I, the decline in schools was very rapid. The marked recovery in the nineteenth century was due to the industrial revolution and the interest of the successful in training children. The qualification was now largely wealth, not ability. As State schools improved, the need to form new public schools declined.

A typical story of one school, now eminently respectable, will show the kind of sequence of events which was happening more or less everywhere. A prosperous Cambridge physician, called Dr Perse, suddenly realised that Cambridge, of all places, had no grammar school. Three days before he died in 1615, having no children, he drew up a will bequeathing a sum of money to be used to found a Cambridge grammar school. To ensure that high standards would be maintained, he stipulated that both the master and the usher should be graduates of Caius College, Cambridge. There were to be 300 free scholars, all fairly local. By the eighteenth century Fellows of Caius College were passing around amongst themselves the offices of Master and Usher of Perse as sinecures. No work was required of them at the school and they robbed the endowment to raise the yearly salaries for each post from £9 to £840. This necessitated reducing the number of free scholars from 300 to fifteen.

Another cause of unscrupulous behaviour, then as now, was the spectacular rise in value of property. For instance, Dulwich College, just south of London, had been founded in 1619, just three years after Perse, as an endowed school with almshouses for the old. There was a spectacular rise in the value of the property, which continues today. The original endowment was £800, but by 1970 it was worth about £18,000. In one of the schools where the boys revolted, they said the masters were not fit to flog them; they hid the key of the cupboard where the birches were kept and said they would do it themselves. Children had no food, and no equipment, sometimes not even tables or benches. As a means of escape, they wandered through the towns in droves. None of the great names were spared this torture. Winchester, Eton, Shrewsbury, Charterhouse, and so on, all so nobly founded, were in this desperate plight. Man's driving force of aggression, through which great deeds can be achieved, split into extreme pathological states of sadism and masochism, which one might call 'floggers and floggees'. Modern research now shows definitely that corporal punishment, as a means of getting children to learn, is a failure. Self-discipline is attained, both over learning and over behaviour, by a suitably graded series of rewards that have meaning to the child. Eventually the student rewards himself by appreciation of the value of learning. Self-discipline is worthwhile for the objective of becoming some kind of specialist, be it carpenter, plumber, doctor, actor, in these or any other areas of achievement.

When the endowed schools fell into such disrepute, it was the boys who took steps to remedy the situation. Intellectually, they were the cream of the land. They began serious revolt, since cries for help were ignored. Schoolmasters had to seek police protection. Public attention was finally won and galvanised into action by a boy at Christ's Hospital, the school founded in 1553 to take little children off the streets of London and protect them. At an upstairs window overlooking the street, where he would be seen by people outside before he was found from inside, he hanged himself. People approached a Member of Parliament known to be interested in education. His name was Brougham (pronounced Broom). A succession of investigations then took place, into charities, into endowed schools, and into education in general. These investigations interested many other men of high calibre.

Rugby, founded in 1567, was a quiet little country school when this wave of violence hit it. There had been a particularly violent revolution in 1826, and a strong character, Dr Arnold, was appointed to take over. He was not a great educator but a very successful university crammer. He helped the boys to discipline themselves sufficiently for the necessary facts to be learned. Rugby soon developed into a place where studies could flourish, and even be enjoyed. St Paul's followed this new attitude by deciding that you must teach boys to study, and then their characters would look after themselves. What the boys should study began to widen out. In the late seventeenth century the merchants had opened a Royal Mathematical Wing at Christ's Hospital, in order that merchant sailors should be trained; and now other schools were including arithmetic with navigation. Charterhouse, founded in 1611, abolished corporal punishment in 1818. New private schools began to include French and arithmetic. The new headmaster of a little country school at Uppingham, Dr Thring, complained that the boy himself had been left out of education. He was a clergyman who had been educated at Eton and, of course, King's College, Cambridge. Life as a boy at Uppingham was more pleasant than it had ever been before at an endowed school. He had the beds partitioned off, which seemed better to him than the bear-garden conditions he recalled from Eton.

The Scots made a move that put them ahead for a century or so. Aberdeen Grammar School, the oldest school in Scotland, had been founded in the thirteenth century, and from that first step other schools developed. After the Reformation the Scots decided that every town must have a school, and each parish must be responsible for both the teacher's salary and the school house. Thus every town was concerned with its own school, and when the decline came, it did not dip so low in Scotland as in England. Altruism for the poor was not forgotten. Hutcheson's, founded in Glasgow in 1643, included twelve poor orphans of Glasgow. An Aberdeen merchant made a fortune in Danzig and returned to found a school for sons and grandsons of hard-up burgesses and merchants of Aberdeen. Loretto, founded in 1827 as a traditional grammar school, was suddenly transformed by a new headmaster, Dr Almond. He was a brilliant scholar and made scientific studies of child growth, dress, diet, and health in general. It was in Scotland that the 'Academy' movement started. This was the foundation of secondary schools of wider interests than the old grammar schools. Morrison's academy at Crieff, founded by a builder in 1818, was for 'the duffusion of useful knowledge', i.e. not just Latin.

With the greater religious tolerance, Ireland (not yet divided) had founded in the north Portora Royal (1608), Royal Belfast (1810) and Campbell College (1894); and in the south St Columba's (1843) and Wesley's college in Dublin (1847). There were also schools in Wales, such as Christ College, Brecon (1541), Monmouth (1614) and Llandovery (1848).

Many of the new schools in this period had religious foundations, but in keeping with the religious tolerance in Britain. John
Wesley founded Kingswood. His regime was very formidable and
he was quite mystified by the outbursts of hysterical weeping
among his pupils that resulted. The children rose at four, summer
and winter, and spent the hour until five in private, partly in
reading, partly in singing, partly in self-examination or medita-
tion, if they were capable of it, Wesley said. He would not even let
the boys go home for the holidays. Roman Catholics who had fled
to France with the dissolution of the monasteries found life so difficult after the French Revolution that they chose to return to
Britain, setting up St Edmund's College and the Jesuit Stonyhurst
by the end of the eighteenth century.

The veritable outbreak of new schools in the nineteenth century
was due to a number of factors. The Industrial Age was again
causing the amassing of private fortunes. Freed from fears for their
survival, the industrialists directed some thoughts to the children.
That Arnold had made Rugby respectable was exactly what they
wanted. They had the money and they were prepared to pay high
fees to have their sons turned into gentlemen. Let the State look
into education for the poor; they wanted their sons to have fee-
paying private education. This elitist development was a vulgar
idea of the newly rich industrialists. It was entirely lacking in the
old merchant altruism of educating poor but able younger sons,
to carry on the work of the community.

Once roused by the Christ's Hospital tragic suicide, the State's
genuine concern showed itself in numerous commissions and in-
quiries. Where an endowed school still did not come up to nine-
teenth-century requirements, it was converted to a State secondary
school. In the mid-1860s, so searching an inquiry was undertaken
by the Endowed Schools Commission that some of the better of
the endowed schools feared that they were all to be swept into the
State system. These headmasters were confident that their schools
were unquestionably better than the State primary and secondary
schools, which were not to differentiate the abler children for
another thirty years. The way in which these better schools managed to withstand pressure to give up their independent status is
best told in Percival, *The Origins of the Headmasters' Conference*

(1969). Briefly, a handful of headmasters called a meeting in 1869 and, with considerable persuasion, managed to get as chairman the distinguished Dr Thring of Uppingham. He did not see that he could have anything to learn from the others, as he had so many fresh ideas of his own. But he was agreeably surprised to find himself impressed by these fellow-headmasters. From 1886 onwards there were annual conferences together. In support of his contention that the human being had been left out, he told of his partitioned beds which gave each boy a private study, of his dislike of mere routine, of the boys' enjoyment of games, handicrafts, art and especially music. He won much support for this widening of the curriculum, and it was to influence State schools also.

But there was no name for these State-resistant schools. By the twentieth century many lists of suggestions were drawn up and thrown away. In 1909 a group of old boys met and called themselves the Public School Club, but their own list was far too short, and schools like St Paul's, Merchant Taylors', Manchester Grammar and Dulwich wanted to know why they were not on the list. Neither the public nor the politicians could make out what these schools were that had escaped becoming State schools. But before the start of the First World War they received a definition: they were schools invited to join the annual Headmasters' Conference. This is still the one qualification, an invitation by the Headmasters' Conference to become members. That, unaided by the State, they had pulled themselves out of the appalling collapse, was indeed praiseworthy. But a more suitable name than 'public' school has still to be selected. Reviewing schools over so many centuries one can, in a way, see how ignorance and misinformation led to the choice of this misnomer by the boys. The Headmasters' Conference was making every effort to dissociate its schools from the disaster schools which had forced the State to intervene. Due to the munificence of the merchants, the endowed schools were, in a manner of speaking, free. They were paid for, not by everyone as in State schools, but by successful merchants; and they were only free to able and male children. In the nineteenth and twentieth centuries, wealth of parents of children in these schools has become of great importance, and it is this fact which negates choice of the word 'public'. Surely, the schools should bear a more appropriate name?

The graph on p. 45 shows such a sharp drop in the number of these schools founded in the twentieth century that the causes should be understood. First, this was partly due to the State schools making steady progress in quality and quantity, with education for all. Secondly, the two World Wars had dissipated many of the fortunes amassed in the Industrial Revolution. Consequently many people felt it quite unnecessary, if not impossible, to pay double fees for their sons, first in rates and taxes, and then in private fees. The idea that it cost less to educate a daughter than a son dates back to when it cost nothing to educate a daughter because they were uneducated, except in the home.

There was yet another blow to the public schools. They really had convinced themselves, and quite a number of other people as well, that only public schools produced men of officer class. But straight away, in the First World War, it was clear to all that the grammar schools were producing excellent officers. However, from the small sample of gifted and talented children described in Chapter 5, we shall see that progressive public schools are making a definite contribution, in accordance with their long history, even dipping into their endowments to aid some who cannot afford the present private fees.

In the nineteenth century the idea that a woman should officially be educated was a revolutionary idea. A few facts will help us to see this in perspective. The State took the first decisive step in 1872, by making education compulsory for girls as well as boys. After that, the old Simon Langton Grammar School, founded in 1575 by Elizabeth I, but which had lapsed, was re-opened again in 1878 for 100 girls as well as 100 boys. The next step was taken by the Mercers' Company. They became aware of the greatly appreciated value of the endowments, and even more of the property of St Paul's School, across the road from St Paul's Cathedral. They decided to move the school to a western suburb of London. The boys moved into the new and impressive premises at Hammersmith in 1884. There was enough money left to found St Paul's Girls' School shortly afterwards. In 1968 the boys moved across the Thames to Barnes, to another impressive building, but not for the girls.

Wykeham of Winchester, as we have seen, had the vision to found a new college at Oxford, still called New College, to which the brightest of the able boys might go to pursue their university studies. Waynflete saw the value of this, and attached Eton to King's College, Cambridge. Subsequently others made direct links between new schools and specific colleges at Oxford or Cambridge. Remembering this, one wonders what opportunities there were for the brightest of the able girls to progress to university studies. At Cambridge, Girton was opened in 1869 and Newnham in 1871; at Oxford, Lady Margaret Hall was opened in 1878 and Somerville in 1879. There was an outcry at the horror of prospective wives being educated, and particularly at having a university education. Any sociologist who cares to look up contemporary newspapers will see the irrational nature of the general response, from almost as many women as men. Students at these women's colleges were called 'blue-stockings' after a group of learned ladies who used to meet for untutored discussions on important topics in a Surrey mansion, because the hostess happened to wear blue stockings from time to time. It was not a good reason for a name, but one does not expect good reasons with irrational reaction.

Very soon after the colleges for women were opened at Cambridge and Oxford, the women were allowed to sit the examinations, but without either the title or the privilege of a degree. Cambridge permitted this much in 1881 and Oxford in 1884. However, full admission to equal status with men in the matter of degrees was not accorded by Oxford until 1920, and not by Cambridge until 1947. London gave women full status with men in 1878, but London University had broken away from Oxford and Cambridge earlier and was looked down on as a nonentity by the older universities. It must be said here that the women were greatly aided in their struggle for academic freedom by many distinguished men.

Enlightened men and women do not want either a patriarchal or a matriarchal society. We have no word for what is required. I have therefore invented one. What we need is an *amphiarchy*, a system in which people, irrespective of sex, have equal opportunity to make their valuable contribution, for which they receive equal recognition from society. The struggle is still acrimonious. As equal pay for equal work progresses to the statute books, the examples of inequality are widely publicised; with nurses under-paid and women less and less willing to be exploited, the hospitals are understaffed, and so on. Incidentally, 'women's lib' is no more to do with casting off clothes than a woman becoming a scholar had anything to do with putting on blue stockings. It is a very handy little title for an extremely important fight to move society towards greater justice. If any woman speaks disparagingly of 'women's lib', one should ask if she has ever voted. Maybe she is too young to have voted and discussion will promote her thinking; maybe she could have voted but never has, and discussion can result in getting her to see that opting out of parliamentary democracy is a negative reaction; and if she has voted, she may be brought to see that this in itself is co-operation with those who in the past struggled to get votes for women. But if anyone argues against 'women's lib', and we wish to try to reorientate that per-son's thinking, it is best to start by defining the term, perhaps as equal opportunity and equal recognition. One has to expect irrational arguments, and it is best to treat each point with extreme calmness.

The pinpricks, which are unimportant but significant, will have to go. For instance, Gardner (1973), in his valuable book *The Public Schools*, gives footnotes of distinguished men who attended the various distinguished schools. Since he mentioned St Paul's Girls School, he might have put a footnote of names such as: Kath-leen Kenyon, CBE, MA, DLit, LHD, FBA, FSA, an archaeologist of great distinction, one-time Principal of St Hugh's College, Oxford, founded 1886; or Baroness Sharp, Permanent Secretary to the Ministry of Housing and Local Government, 1955–6; or Imogen Holst, musician in her own right, as well as daughter of Gustav Holst; or Celia Johnson, OBE, actress of distinction and wife of Peter Fleming; or Shirley Williams, MP. As personalities, such women are far too big to care whether they are in anybody's footnotes or not. The significance of such pinpricks is that they are indications of whether minds are becoming oriented to the concept of amphiarchy or not. There are books from which one can obtain information on the very considerable achievements of women after little over a century of education. One of the latest at the time of writing is the Centenary Book produced in 1974 by the Association of Headmistresses, with the felicitous title of *Reluctant Revolutionaries*.

The break-up of any system of society is always alarming for the established authorities, be the change from religious to secular schools, from one sex education to education for all, or from educating only the brightest to educating children at all levels of ability. Each time society has one of these volcanic eruptions to achieve a step towards what is believed to be greater fairness, the 'prophets of doom' are undergoing greater insecurity than they are able to tolerate. Greater opportunity and recognition for women is one such social upheaval for the men, and particularly for young husbands and young fathers, that is to say men who have only just taken on family responsibilities. Women could, perhaps, brief themselves on the contribution of great men of a century ago who gave definitive assistance to women in their fight for equality. This is a way to win the men's involvement in the campaign. One example must suffice. When what one might call the 'blue-stocking battle' was at its most virulent, the great Jewish humanist scholar, Claude Montefiore, saw that women should be given the opportunity to study in peace, away from the storms about women's colleges at Oxford and Cambridge. He gathered some enlightened men and women, and held their committee meetings near St Paul's, Hammersmith, at the house of a woman who had six sons at that school but no peaceful college to which to send her daughter. Before the end of the nineteenth century they opened the Froebel Educational Institute in Colet Gardens, with considerable financial help from Claude Montefiore. The studies were to include understanding of young children, so the Frobel Demonstration School was opened.

The son of one of those six sons attended the Demonstration School at the age of four in 1910, together with other little children who were subsequently to achieve distinction. He gave the following account of his most vivid impressions. First, the beautiful old Froebelian three-dimensional geometric forms of a sphere, a cube and a cone, set out on the mantelpiece; then that the teachers were not angry when he accidentally wet his pants, but gave him a book to read (he could read at four), while they washed and dried the pants; and lastly how he fell deeply in love with one beautiful teacher who answered all his questions. That was not typical of schools in 1910. The Froebel Institute, as it is now called, has moved out to Roehampton. Miss Brearley, Principal in the 1960s, was a member of the committee for the Plowden Report on children and primary schools, produced in 1967.

During the years since then, with the State system of education progressing in both quality and quantity, for girls as well as boys, the interaction of the dual system of private and State education has produced a most constructive dialogue. Each system outstripped the other in some ways; and what one system said was impossible, the other made efforts to prove perfectly feasible. The London County Council had introduced care for the gifted in 1893 by the old selection methods; but within ten years news of Binet's work, with its remarkable invention of a formula for mental age, reached Britain. The young Cyril Burt visited Paris, and spent some weeks in Professor Wundt's laboratory at Leipzig, the first experimental psychological laboratory ever to be established. When the London County Council appointed Burt, no one there was interested in intelligence tests; they just wanted him to discover the children so lacking in ability that special provision must be made for them. But the young man who was later to set up the first department of statistical psychology ever to be established, quietly noted those children at the other end of the normal distribution of intelligence, the gifted boys and girls. From that time onward, both here and in the United States, assessment of intelligence became increasingly more reliable than the old method of selection solely by ability to decode the alphabet.

When today comprehensive schools are discussed, presumably this refers to socio-economic status. No one has made the retrograde suggestion that educationally subnormal children should be withdrawn from their more suitable special schools and put back in schools for normal children. Whether there should be special schools for the intellectually brilliant children is a matter for further research. Information on that is not yet available for making such a decision. Undoubtedly Sir Robert Blair of the London County

Council must be counted amongst the outstanding professional men who aid women's struggle for equality of opportunity, not only by improving education in general but also by introducing the scholarship system for both sexes.

Today, areas of the mind to be studied and suitable ways to improve the curriculum are broadening. In addition to levels of intellectual giftedness, levels of artistic talent, as described in Chapter 4, are increasingly borne in mind. What should never be lost sight of is Sir Robert Blair's 1893 reminder: *what must be done must be regardless of wealth, influence or social class.*

3

THE ASSESSMENT OF INTELLIGENCE

People have probably always wondered how the mind works, ever since it became sufficiently complex to reflect upon itself; that is to say, ever since there were humans. With the coming of education for all, it was much easier to examine the minds of children of all classes. Teachers were now being trained to teach, but alphabetic reading was still a major factor in judging the level of ability of the children. Towards the end of the nineteenth century a French professor began to reverse the age-old process. Instead of imposing learning upon the children, to see if they could take it, he began to question them on general matters, and listened to their replies in order to see how their minds worked.

At the turn of the century Professor Binet, Psychologist at the Sorbonne in Paris, was keeping careful notes about the way in which his two daughters answered questions which he put to them. In 1903 he published a report of this experimental study of the intellect which was widely read in the Western world. Both girls were clearly bright but they tackled the questions in quite different ways. The French Government had just followed the British in making school compulsory. Binet was asked if he would discover for them the answer to the one problem which besets every teacher: which are the children who can't work and which the ones who won't work.

Binet went into the Paris schools and asked children the questions he had put to his daughters. Sometimes he would spend half a day or more with one child. He very soon came across a puzzling situation. There were a handful of children who answered questions at about the same ages as his daughters had been able to answer them. But the great majority had to be older before they knew the answers; and some could not answer the questions even when they were old enough to leave school. While Binet was thinking this over, he had the sudden insight which put twentieth-century intelligence-testing on its scientific road. He proposed that besides having a chronological age, a child also has a mental age, which may or may not be the same as the chronological age.

That was Binet's great contribution, and the insight came to him through asking children questions based on how minds work. Just to underline his invention, imagine a new airport in a country district. In the local school there are two groups of children: the local 'country bumpkins' and the newly arrived children of technicians and scientists attached to the airport. Go into the twelve-year-old class. The chronological age is, say, twelve years to twelve years eleven months. This is quite a small range. But the mental age can be from about eight years to perhaps eighteen years. Some of the children cannot climb very high on the ladder of questions; others can climb almost to the top; but the great majority climb to somewhere in the middle of the ladder.

It was customary at that time, and still is, for doctors to express various aspects of a child's development in terms of a relation or ratio between the individual child's developmental stage of bone or height or muscular co-ordination and what is normal or average development for that age. The best way to express this relation or ratio is the customary mathematical one of a fraction, with the child's score of successful answers at the top and his chronological age at the bottom. Nobody knows who first thought of this way of expressing the intelligence fraction or ratio. It was the obvious thing to do and probably quite a number of psychologists set the intelligence quotient down in this way, without actually copying anyone else. So 'intelligence quotient' means no more than 'intelligence answer' when mental age is related to chronological age. The formula was now invented for relating an individual child's intellectual capacity to that of the majority of children of the same chronological age. But a funny little human quirk refused to let it rest there. When the top number is the same as the bottom number, the answer is one; when the top number is more than the bottom number, the answer is more than one; and when the top number is less than the bottom one, the answer is less than one. Some people, probably quite mistakenly, thought parents of intellectually below-average children would be affronted at being told that their child's intelligence was less than one. So the fraction was subjected to a perfectly legitimate mathematical treatment: the top and bottom of the fraction were multiplied by 100. Thus, using initials for chronological and mental age, the formula becomes: $\dfrac{MA}{CA}$ x 100. Once the letters are replaced by figures, the quotient can be worked out.

Let us say there are three boys of exactly ten, neither a month more nor a month less. They all have the same number at the bottom of their formula. But they all have quite different mental ages, so each top figure will be different. Tom has mental age five years. Dick has mental age ten years. Harry has mental age fifteen years. To state the answer of their intelligence level, the quotient of their intelligence, this is how it must be worked out:

Tom	$\dfrac{5}{10}$	x	100	=	IQ 50
Dick	$\dfrac{10}{10}$	x	100	=	IQ 100
Harry	$\dfrac{15}{10}$	x	100	=	IQ 150

Always remember that the fixed chronological age goes at the bottom and the mental age goes at the top, where it may be larger or smaller than the bottom number.

At the beginning of the century, psychology had only just broken loose from philosophy. Actually the word 'psychology' was invented by Aristotle but the philosophers suppressed it for some two thousand years. Psychologists went to the children and found out what kinds of puzzles they liked solving. Comics had been published for a decade in Britain and they looked at the questions, jokes, mazes and so on that children enjoyed. The philosophical and psychological approaches were fused in questions planned to cover as many mental processes as possible *in forms which the children would enjoy.*

The United Kingdom and the United States were extremely fortunate in having two brilliant young psychologists attracted to Binet's work in France. They were just embarking on careers which were to prove more than half a century long. In London, Dr Cyril Burt, just down from Cambridge, published his first paper on the experimental study of intelligence in 1909; and in California Dr Lewis Terman was appointed to the staff of his own University of Stanford, which is just south of San Francisco. Burt saw at once that we should never get enough information about all the children's level of intelligence, working only through individual tests. So he compiled the first group test and tried it out on London children, having trained the teachers to administer the test. Terman made a detailed revision of Binet's questions, covering a greater range of mental processes, and this became known as the Stanford–Binet Intelligence Scale. It first appeared in 1916; then it was revised again in 1937 and yet again in 1960.

How can one be sure that these questions, fitted roughly to mental processes, should normally be answered at one age rather than another? First, let us consider the various types of questions. All these types, based on how the mind is thought to work, are arranged in short ladders, and the child climbs each one to as high a level as he can. Here are some examples:

1   The child has to retain in consciousness enough figures or words to work out problems; so from small child to brilliant adult (judged by MA) the digits to be repeated run from 2 to 9, and the sentences have from two to fifteen words (approximately). The children just have to repeat a set of figures or a sentence.

2   Logic is more amusing to identify if presented in the form of an illogical story or picture: e.g. 'Bobby Thompson has an axe so heavy that he cannot lift it. So he only cuts down very big trees.' The difficulty of these logical problems progresses to fit an increase of mental age.

3   The vocabulary is assessed by lists of words that grow harder and harder, and also more abstract.

There are many other thought processes of the mind which are tested by means of these short series of ladders, the variety of purposes grouped together in what are called batteries of tests. Optimum working is easiest with individual tests, such as the Stanford–Binet Scale and the Wechsler Intelligence Scale for Children (WISC).

As already pointed out in the previous chapter, some children do not do their best reasoning through words. Therefore another series for assessing mental age makes the minimum use of words. For instance, a child may be presented with a picture of a line of ducks with one chicken in the row, and he or she is asked to put a ring round the odd one. The questions have to be as surprising and entertaining to the child as each fresh issue of a comic paper. This often gives a wrong impression of secrecy. The above logical problem of Bobby Thompson is not in any test. If it were, a child might hear about it, and even be given the answer by someone who had read this book. It is a matter of professional etiquette not to inform the public as to what questions will be asked.

The tests that are arranged in these little series of ladders, to see how high in mental processes a child can climb, are not composed of just any questions. Each one is carefully structured and standardised. With tests involving the recall of a series of random numbers, a random table is used to ensure that no human bias towards a particular sequence of numbers is exhibited by the person presenting the test.

Research workers go out to present these tests to a wide variety of schools and return with information about how many digits a child of six, six and a half, six and three-quarters, seven years, and so on, can repeat. A thousand children at each quarter-year, all the way up to adult, should be tested. In order to standardise the tests, at least a thousand children in each age group (grouped in quarter-years) need to be tested in order to provide a reliable measure of intelligence for age. Every kind of question, from those for the small child to those for the brilliant adult, need to be standardised in this way. About three-quarters of a particular age have to succeed for the question-and-answer to be accepted. If *everyone* of one age could answer it, it would be too easy; and if *nobody* of that same age could answer it, it would be too hard.

When somebody asks if a test has been standardised, this is a very important question. Only standardised questions of this kind can give genuine estimates of mental age for the intelligence quotient formula. Anyone who takes a course on testing finds that there is a great deal more than this to learn. But at least we can now see how the formula for IQ was invented, how the questions were planned to fit the way the mind works, and how every single question has to be standardised. Mental age will only be revealed by standardised questions applied when the child is at ease and working happily at his or her optimum level.

Many educationists find it difficult to step aside from their teaching role in order to give a psychological test and some cannot refrain from giving the child too much help. The successful educational psychologist is a well-qualified, sensitive, intuitive person who can persuade a child to relax so that he or she enjoys solving amusing puzzles. What one is after is not examination-maximum effort but optimum response. It makes no difference where in the scale of intelligence the child comes, so long as there emerges a true picture of the way a particular child's mind works. This is completely different from the 'sleeves-up' strenuous efforts of a good educator to lead the child's thinking by one rephrased question after another. Only the standardised question may be asked in the IQ test, nothing more. If the child lacks confidence, this is built up by a warm response to successful answers. If the child is over-confident, attention may be drawn to an unnecessary failure, as a sobering experience. But most of the time every answer is accepted with appreciation. If one just says 'Good' or 'Good try' in the right way, the child need not have the depressing experience of failure which interferes with optimum working. With such skilled effort to maintain equilibrium, one may not, while working, suspect that a very gifted child is doing unusually well.

So there is indeed a scientific way of approaching children's varying levels of intelligence, which is more reliable than the views of individual teachers or parents. Most people would agree that a good teacher is a good judge of children. But the striking fact is that the good teachers, right from the start of standardised testing, have been the first to praise the value of objective measures. Mostly, the way they ranked the children coincided with the test results.

But there were a few surprises, and it was after giving more intellectual stimulus to the occasional bright child whose work was not outstanding that they were finally convinced of the great contribution that these tests could make.

One has to view the storms that blow up in the newspapers on the IQ debate with a touch of cynicism. The reports represent battles on two levels. On the one hand journalists provide extensive and general coverage on a non-professional level. On the other hand, the experts are engaged in debate at a sophisticated and specialised level. However, at both levels one can scarcely fail to notice that the debate on heredity and environment is frequently mentioned as a cause of dissension. Both are always present. Of course heredity and environment are the major determinants but the debate as to their relative importance continues.

A constructive analogy is to compare the distribution of intelligence with the distribution of height. Most people are of more or less medium height, some a little more and some a little less; but there are a few who are extremely tall and a few who are extremely short. That is so with a homogeneous group, though there are complications if one compares small Celtic people with tall Nordic people. By and large, height is a good analogy except for one point: on the whole women are shorter than men, but there is no difference between men and women in the distribution of intelligence. The myth that women are less intelligent as well as shorter received a death-blow with objective testing. Suppose a child is born of very tall parents, we can expect that child to grow tall, if not very tall. Now suppose that that child is born into a very poor environment. Bad housing, poor feeding, insufficient sleep, anxiety about money, and so on, can severely affect the child. He may grow up weakly, with undeveloped muscles and poor co-ordination. But his height will be almost unaffected. He may be an inch or so shorter than he would have been with proper care; but if he was going to be tall he would still grow into a tall adult. Much the same is true on the intellectual side. Deprive the child of proper intellectual stimulus, and his mind will work less well.

One of the delights of educational journalism has been to find experiments which suggest that 'IQ has been raised'. Tests are not faultless, nor are administrators, so there is a confusion here between actual heredity (which cannot be changed after conception) and environment. Environment can be changed; and what is more, society must change it radically in the interests of the underprivileged. Instead of grumbling about so large a 'middle class', let us congratulate ourselves that environment has improved for so many. This is the group which has to show wisdom by concerning itself with the problem of the so-called 'poverty gap'. If the answer is a fairer distribution of wealth, then the fortunate sector should be the one to insist that due steps are taken to repair this situation (though it may lessen the wealth of some of them). Altruism and egoism are part of human nature, and full development requires balance of both innate forces.

It is very likely that many problems are most likely to be solved by our most able citizens. But their training in wisdom has to begin early. Let us first look at the distribution of all intelligence before focusing on our particular concern, the top 2 to 3 per cent of children.

Table 2   DISTRIBUTION OF IQS OF THE 1937 STANDARDISATION GROUP

IQ	%	Classification
160–169	0·03	Very Superior
150–159	0·2	
140–149	1·1	
130–139	3·1	Superior
120–129	8·2	
110–119	18·1	High Average
100–109	23·5	Normal or average
90–99	23·0	
80–89	14·5	Low Average
70–79	5·6	Borderline Defective*
60–69	2·0	Mentally Defective
50–59	0·4	
40–49	0·2	
30–39	0·03	

Source: Terman, L. M. and Merrill, M.A. (1961).

* We no longer use the term 'Defective' but say 'Below average' for IQ 70–79 and 'Educationally Subnormal' for IQ 69 to about 50.

From Table 2 we can see that nearly 80 per cent of the population has average (including high and low average) intelligence. Before leaving the total distribution we should note that many of the schools for children below IQ 70 are regarded with great pride. They are called special schools and the well-cared-for children in good ones are rightly proud to go to 'my special school'. The children blossom with the imaginative care given to them. The head usually points out at least one 'little genius who should not be here at all' on account of an IQ that has turned out to be well into the 70s and 80s. They nearly always conclude by saying they are not mentioning this because they do not want to part with these relatively bright children. The lowest forms of our normal schools are rarely so appreciated, though their IQs are also often in the 70s or 80s. Some might question whether it is fair to hold back children with IQs in the 70s and 80s. The apparent rise has taken place because they were removed from normal to special school. Statistical psychology is one of our tools; but individual children have to be treated according to their own circumstances.

By definition, in the United Kingdom and the United States children with IQ over 130 are now called gifted. From Table 3 we can see that this is just under 3 per cent. When results are over 169 we usually say IQ 170+. This is because not enough children have been found who are so gifted intellectually that we have been able to standardise tests for them satisfactorily. But there are twelve times as many as we once thought with IQ over 170. This has been demonstrated through psychological statistics. The UK and USA bring out jointly a *Year Book of Education* and the 1962 edition was on the gifted child. Table 3 gives the distribution of gifted children as agreed between the two countries.

Table 3 DISTRIBUTION OF GIFTED INTELLIGENCE

IQ	%	
Above 130	2·25	1 in 44
Above 140	0·55	1 in 180
Above 150	0·14	1 in 700
Above 160	0·034	1 in 2,900

Source: Year Book of Education, 1962.

With primary school classes the size they are in the UK, every teacher should expect to find one gifted child and be prepared to give the extra help which will stretch the gifted child's mind. Alas, this is impossible unless the words of the Plowden Report (1967) are taken to heart and at least some of the day is arranged for individual children to work on their own.

The next question that comes to mind is: *where do all the gifted children come from?* Are they all the children of professors? Indeed, no. For one thing that would require 2 or 3 per cent of the population to be professors. There are nothing like as many professors as this. Furthermore, professors are not renowned for marrying lady professors. This touches on the problem of heredity. It is exasperating to work from the Registrar General's Classification of Fathers' Occupations, because this indicates only half the heredity. So long as marriage is a matter of free choice, young people will marry for many reasons and whether they choose someone of about the same intellectual level is not usually a top priority. However, the Registrar General's classification is the best indication of social level and therefore ability that we have so far; and most researchers adapt it to suit their own purposes.

The following is a rough and ready indication: gifted children come from all classes. But only 1 per cent have fathers who are labourers. More come from the partly skilled and skilled classes. Still more come from the lower professional group, but there the increase stops. There are far too few people in the highest professional group for them to produce many children, gifted or otherwise. However, there is a sliding scale if we are looking for very high IQs such as over 150. These we are more likely to find in the professional classes; and as there are many more fathers in the lower professional classes, we shall find some of the highest IQs there too.

Burt (1961) found so many gifted children who did not come from the most cultured homes that he made a special study. As already stated, he found: Gauss (son of a bricklayer); Laplace (son of a farm labourer); Marlowe and James Mill (sons of cobblers); James Watt, Lincoln and Carlyle (sons of carpenters); Franklin (son of a soap-boiler); Kepler (son of an innkeeper); and

Kant (son of a strapmaker). So we have to be open-minded in our search for gifted children. Our task is to discover them wherever they are.

In 1970 the results of very extensive population research under the direction of Redcliffe-Maud were published in *Reform of Local Government in England*. England was divided into eight Provinces, as shown on the map (p. 68). Size of population for each area was given, both exact for 1968 and projected for 1981. The latest census at that time was that of 1961; this stated that in 1961 there were 11½ million children, aged 0–15 years. If we combine these two sets of figures with the percentages of gifted children (Table 3) we get a projectile of how many gifted children to expect in the eight Provinces of England. These are set out in Table 4. Let the reader take any Province of particular interest to him and see what numbers of gifted children aged 0–15 years should be expected there. The local education authorities will thus be able to estimate just how many children with IQ above 160 are to be expected in their various areas. Throughout England we should assume that there are, in schools, 1,500 of a level of intelligence which the schools could not possibly cope with on their own. We should, strictly speaking, include those with IQ over 150 if not also those over 140. Schools should be able to adapt the syllabus for children of IQ 131–139.

Since the 1961 Census there has been another one, the 1971 Census. The predicted population increase by 1981 (final column, Table 4) is on its way. The 46+ million people in England has already become 40·5 million. So our figures already significantly underestimate the situation. Present-day educational planning should always bear in mind estimates for the *next* census. Population changes can be seen in *Whitaker's Almanack*. There, the steady rise, from 1801 when the census began, to today, can be seen under *Population*. Even a relatively sparsely populated area, such as East Anglia, should prepare for about 184 children with IQ over 160 by the 1980s.

In the United States, preparations for the gifted and artistically talented, along such lines of prediction, are already going on. Some of this work is described in the final chapter. But we have not yet set out in single-minded search for those we would train to become

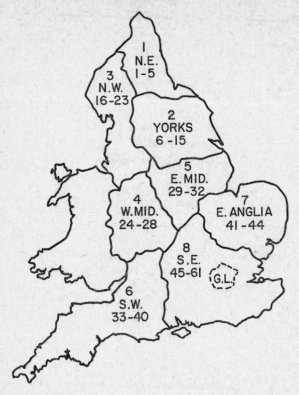

our wise leaders. Let us try to make an imaginative leap from the information we have so far. The north of England is frequently described as a depressed area, because, so it is said, all the promising people are trying to move to the south-east, to the London area. Children in the north tend to leave school earlier, the implication being that the north is left with little 'sixth form material', by which is meant children of sixteen to eighteen years worth preparing for the university. Whether or not the people in the south-east have on average a slightly higher level of intelligence, neither area is discovering its able children with any thoroughness. From Table 4 we can, for instance, work out how many exceptionally gifted children are to be expected in the north-east, north-west and Yorkshire provinces together. Between them, they should now be

Table 4 ESTIMATED DISTRIBUTION OF GIFTED CHILDREN IN ENGLAND

Areas		Provinces	Estimated population in thousands (k)		Estimated no of children with IQ above				Expected % increase 1981
			1968	1981	130	140	150	160	%
1	1–5	North-east	2,749k	2,926k	15,000	3,700	900	230	+6
2	6–15	Yorkshire	4,849k	5,271k	27,000	6,500	1,700	400	+9
3	16–23	North-west	6,999k	7,640k	38,000	9,400	2,400	580	+9
4	24–28	West Midlands	5,164k	5,803k	28,000	6,900	1,900	430	+12
5	29–32	East Midlands	3,017k	3,372k	17,000	4,000	1,000	250	+12
6	33–40	South-west	4,061k	4,515k	22,000	5,400	1,400	370	+11
7	41–44	East Anglia	1,990k	2,391k	11,000	2,700	700	170	+20
8	45–61	South-east							
		less Greater London	9,289k	10,929k	51,000	12,500	3,100	770	+18
		Greater London only	7,764k	7,623k	43,000	10,400	2,700	640	−2 decr.
		Province 8 Total	17,053k	18,552k	94,000	22,900	5,800	1,410	+9 incr.

Sources: Reform of Local Government in England (London, 1970); Areas, Provinces, populations, 1968, 1981. Year Book of Education: The Gifted Child (London and New York, 1962); percentages of gifted children. 1961 Census for England and Wales; 47,135,510 people, 11,506,000 of whom (24·4 per cent) were aged 0–15 years.

looking for some 80,000 gifted children (apart from the talented); and what is more, over 1,200 of them (a conservative estimate) should have IQs higher than 160. It does not matter whether the south-east has more. What matters is who is going to start educating these children suitably. The north could well take a lead here, if it had the enterprise. As a matter of fact, one of the first government-sponsored researches on the education of gifted children was conducted in the north, at Liverpool, under Professor Tempest. The findings of this are being taken a step further by the NAGC which is sponsoring a follow-up.

From Table 5, we can see the decline in wealth of the top 10 per cent of the population (first three columns) and the rise in wealth

Table 5　WEALTH DISTRIBUTION

Percentage of wealth for individuals in Great Britain aged over twenty-four

		Top 1% of well-to-do (5 and 4 star)	Next 4% of well-to-do (3 star)	Next 5% of well-to-do (2 star)	Rest
A	*Inland Revenue basis*				
	1911–13	69	18	5	8
	1924–30	62	22	6	9
	1936–8	56	23	9	12
	1954	43	28	8	21
	1960	42	33	8	17
	1965	32	26	13	29
	1973	23	24	16	37
B	*'Corrected' Basis (excluding State Pension Rights)*				
	1965	29	25	13	33
	1973	19	19	14	48
C	*'Corrected' basis (including State Pension Rights)*				
	1965	22	19	11	48
	1973	14	16	11	59

Source: Alan Day, 'The nation's wealth: who owns it?' Observer (20 January 1974).

of the rest (last column). The fair distribution of wealth is one of the tasks which our politicians have not yet solved. The profligate debtor still gains while the honest saver loses. It is imperative that we find and prepare the leaders of the future who are capable of solving such problems with wisdom. Parents of gifted children should demand that teachers are equipped to direct help to these children, for the good of all, even if it means calling in specialists. Parents and teachers have repeatedly to draw attention to the fact that it is statutory in the 1944 Education Act that children are to be taught according to their ability and aptitude. The move towards attaining this objective is complex, involving many people and many organisations, but at least the twentieth century has brought us far more reliable ways of identifying intellectual ability.

4

THE VALUE OF ART

Art does not lend itself to objective assessment in the same way as intelligence. A measure of objectivity can be obtained but on quite a different principle. Where reasoning can proceed along a clear pathway in consciousness, both the creation and the appreciation of art are concerned with the work of art as a whole. Thus, for the assessment of intelligence it is possible to standardise questions covering all aspects of intelligence and give a child a mental age according to the age of most children at that child's level of ability; and the mental age is then related to the child's chronological age. But the complexity of a whole personality, covering temperament, individual powers of perception through all the senses, innate and environmental influences, as well as intellectual gifts, has not lent itself yet to any simple formula. Experiments have been tried over three-quarters of a century without success. At times success seemed near, both here and in the United States, only to resolve itself into the factor of intelligence which was being assessed. In the States they now use the word 'gifted' in connection with intelligence, and reserve 'talented' for the varying artistic abilities; and that is the way the two words are used here.

There are great differences in individual perception through the various senses. One may be acutely aware of music but insensitive to painting; another may be acutely aware of movement but untouched by sculpture. At the end of his television series on art, Lord Clark said it had given him great pleasure to choose suitable music. Clearly he was sensitive to music as well as to painting and sculpture. Professor Burt was extremely non-visual but able to hear a whole Mozart opera from reading the score, even increasing or decreasing numbers of individual instruments to find the desired balance. On one occasion he conducted an experiment on appreciation of pictures. He got a wide range of people, from cultured to low socio-economic homes, to rank ten pictures in order of beauty. The pictures ranged from most beautiful to unaesthetic in the extreme. The one who ranked them in exactly the same order as the Director of the Royal Academy was a Lyons Nippy waitress. Professor Burt then repeated the experiment with different pictures. This time they were not identical, but very near. From this and other experiments he concluded that aesthetic appreciation was innate, as well as teachable.

Throughout the history of art, the opinion of an expert in any medium has been accepted as the best possible judgement obtainable. Psychologists have devised a method which can be more objective than the opinion of one person. Two or three experts in a medium, such as painting, ballet, drama or music, can discuss together the salient points they are looking for; and when they have come to some agreement they work independently and compare notes afterwards. If their independent judgements agree, the results can be regarded as objective. Statistical treatment of such experiments shows that having more than three people making the judgements does not increase objectivity. The operative point is that the two or three are in agreement as to what they are expecting of the artist or the work of art. Therefore we must look at the nature of various arts from the standpoint of forming reliable opinions, as the talents of children have to be encouraged.

'Aesthetic' means belonging to the appreciation of the beautiful. People who are very sensitive aesthetically report a sense of shock when first contemplating great art, be it painting, music, drama or any of the arts. Early in the twentieth century researchers thought out an ingenious experiment regarding pictures. Beside some of the pictures in an exhibition they concealed a small camera. They compared the recordings in film with what people actually said they had experienced. There was a definite connection between those who said they had felt a shock and the film of them, which revealed various indications of shock. The pupils dilated, and this is the most difficult of all reflexes to control; breathing increased in speed and this effect lasted from thirty seconds to five minutes in different individuals.

Any experience which affects the endocrinal system in this way must be biological in origin. Indeed, it now seems that aesthetic experience in general has a biological origin, which means that though some appear innately or environmentally much more developed aesthetically, aesthetic experience is born in us all to some degree. The deep origin is the state of shock when endocrinal stimulus, such as adrenalin, pours through the body to such an extent that the body cannot cope with it, and the awareness of what is happening seems to put a gulf between the person having the experience and the real experience which has so roused him. Certain highly sensitive temperaments are particularly subject to this state of detachment. What, in biological terms, should make them react quickly in either attack or flight, is in excess of what such people can tolerate and they detach themselves in this way, like a dreamer watching a fearful nightmare situation, or an audience watching *King Lear*. Indeed, the whole history of drama exploits this state, which as a biological mechanism is a failure.

The following incident, related to the author, may make the biological failure clear. A brilliant young scientist was studying animals and plants in the African jungle, carrying a gun in case it should be necessary. Suddenly a lion sprang at him through the trees. He lifted his gun but there was no time to pull the trigger. He had that peculiar feeling of parting company with himself. From the time the lion appeared, through the descent upon him, he thought it was all happening very slowly, though the rush of adrenalin and other secretions to his brain was actually causing him to think very fast. He was thrown back by the weight of the lion, and his gun hit the ground. He thought, 'So this is what it is like when a man is killed by a lion', as if he were watching a drama. He had no feeling of fear. There was time to wonder why the lion never reached him, but it was some moments before he realised that the butt of his gun had wedged on the ground in such a way that the barrel had gone clean through the lion's brain. There are many stories from travellers in danger of this curious sense of coming adrift, a state of schizophrenia, which by derivation means divided mind.

In a crude pantomime all the children scream of the villain, 'There he is! Behind you!' In a nursery class, the children join in

with the repetitions they so love in a story. But adults have usually
had long training in dividing their behaviour and their experience
of art. When King Richard cries 'My kingdom for a horse !', half
the people in the stalls may own horses but it is only the old
farmers' wife in the gallery who nudges her husband and says,
'George ! Can't we let him have the old grey mare?' Thus we can
see that sophisticated reaction to art emerges from skilled practice
as well as innate disposition. Because of the heightened awareness
of the whole in aesthetic experience, it is a major factor in achieving integrity of personality. Both the appreciation – now known
to be a primary experience in its own right – and the creation of
art are now recognised as essential ingredients of integrity. So important is aesthetic experience that men and women risk their lives
for the truth they see in art, just as they risk their lives for the truth
they see in science.

Mikis Theodorakis is a first-class composer of Greek songs and
has always been politically very aware. In the *bouzouki taverna*,
which are small Greek restaurants, he sang to his own accom-
paniment these charming songs, to earn his living but also to do
much more. He put the bitter history of Greece into these songs
and only those who paid attention noted the political implications. For a while his intent was only noticed by his friends and
of course they did not report him. But soon the numbers who
flocked to hear him were noticed by friends of the military junta,
who reported him. He was imprisoned yet again. The following
incident, which he was able to describe later, gives some indication of the suffering of a family with a member imprisoned for
singing the truth. When his father visited him for what they took
to be their last meeting, the trial dossier had arrived. The father
looked down and saw that the penalty for the alleged offence was
death and had been underlined. 'They have underlined it in red
in case we should miss it,' laughed Theodorakis uncertainly. His
father knew the utter despair that had seized Theodorakis in
recent weeks. 'He dropped his glasses,' said Theodorakis later,
'and looked me straight in the eyes.' In a strong but calm, solemn
voice, he said: 'Death on the battlefield, my child, is a normal
thing for a Theodorakis. Remember your great-great-grandfather, Khalis: he was at the head of the first insurrection against

the Turks in Crete. Your other great-great-grandfather, Spydirakis, was impaled by the Turks. Your uncle, Mandis, was skinned alive. Your father faced the Turks at Bizanti fort when he was sixteen. Well, you'll only be following in the heroic family tradition. If they kill you, you will have my blessing . . .'[1]

With death so imminent, what could have saved him? His family and friends, feeling his dangerously deep despair, persuaded him to make up more songs and whisper them through the bars without the guards noticing. By means of brave friends these songs were flown to the United States and Broadcast, then to the United Kingdom, and finally to the whole world. Theodorakis was now a greater danger confined than free, so he was let out of prison.

Solzhenitsyn's search for truth is in literature, and he wished to communicate it in his own country. This intellectual giant has been imprisoned and tortured many times. Many of the people he met in prison were creative people of the highest calibre, and they had long discussions on the nature of being, and the unbridled cruelty that breaks through when people lack integrity. His Nobel Speech on Literature, 'One word of truth . . .', is available at any bookshop in English and/or Russian in pamphlet form. This is how it opens:

As the savage, confronted with a strange object, asks himself, was it cast up by the ocean? Has it been long buried in the sand? Did it fall from the sky? – an intricately curved object, reflecting the light now dimly, now with flashing brilliance – turns it this way and that in bewilderment, twists it, tries to adapt it to some purpose, seeks to find some lowly acceptable use for it, never suspecting its high purpose, so we too, holding Art in our hands, conceitedly deem ourselves its masters. . . .

He quotes Dostoevsky as saying, 'The world will be saved by beauty.' Genuine artistic work, Solzhenitsyn goes on, is utterly convincing. Works drawing on truth compel us even centuries later. Art, he says, re-creates situations for the individual to make

[1] Quoted in Melina Mercouri, *I Was Born Greek.*

the experiences his own; Dostoevsky, in *Possessed*, foresaw the hijackings and the hostages planned to destroy civilisation. In conclusion, Solzhenitsyn states that violence exists on a lie. It is only collapsed and overcome by the one word of 'truth' which can outweigh the whole world.

If men can risk their lives in this way, seeking truth as rigorously as in any scientific investigation through media such as song and literature, those who have failed to grasp the integrative importance of art must not be allowed to hold us back.

We now have in the United Kingdom an Arts Council. Once a month twenty unpaid eminences meet in London. There is a permanent staff of some 250 to carry out their decisions. The activities range from art exhibitions, drama, and literature to experimental work with young people's theatre, dance and jazz. In the early 1970s a new department of regional development was initiated, each area with its own director and committee. All this costs money, but what men pay money for they respect. In 1971/2 these activities cost nearly £12 million and the following year the price had gone up to over £17 million. Nobody could say we are totally neglecting the arts. Without this financial assistance there would certainly be no Covent Garden, Royal Ballet (Sadler's Wells), or National Theatre, in London. Where we have to wage war is not against other nations but against the notions in our midst which cause people to refer to art as unproductive. If we do not give the artist his due place in society, it is integrity and wisdom that we are slighting.

So great an organisation as the Arts Council is bound to run into problems endemic in bureaucracy. Both artists and appreciators have to be eternally vigilant for objectives to be attainable. An attack was published in 1974 in *Patronage of the Creative Artist*, from Artists Now. This report was drawn up by a panel of five: two have served on Arts Council panels and committees; one is an author and playwright who has organised workshops and concerts; one is a painter; and one is a composer who was founder of the Redcliffe Concerts of British Music. It attacks the Arts Council very hard, sometimes unfairly. But its real value lies in suggestions as to what should be done. They think that the unpaid eminences should meet the artists and their work face to face, and not allow hundreds, of whom they never hear, to be turned away by officials of bureaucracy. They want an opportunity for the public, who pay the rates and taxes by which the Arts Council is financed, to meet the many hundreds who are turned away, so that they can make known their appreciations. Actually, the Council of Artists which they suggest might well fall into the very errors which they condemn in the panels and committees of the Arts Council, if it flourished. Moreover, this leaves out the appreciators who, though not mighty patrons, constitute the bulk of support in the various arts. The writers of this extremely interesting report do not get down to the problems of selection. They should strive for greater objectivity, as for instance suggested with the small panels of independent judges, who meet first for discussion of criteria, and then assess the work, or art, or performance, on their own. If the Arts Council is to survive as a viable body, there have to be many more such attacks, and we must hope that they are as valuable as this one for discussion. Such constructive criticism is the only way to keep a great organisation like the Arts Council from decaying through unpruned growth.

Both artist and public, which constitutes the main body of appreciators, have to maintain a delicate balance between being receptive to new ideas and critical of them. Innovations may or may not have worth; and in order to make up one's mind it is absolutely necessary to give sympathetic attention. It is also extremely helpful to hear well-informed critics, but critics and artists alike have to avoid becoming too specialised, as this may jeopardise the whole for the sake of a part. Broadcasting in 1973 on Gombrich's *Symbolic Images*, Michael Podro, at that time at the University of Essex, said: 'Sir Ernst Gombrich, Director of the Warburg Institute, breaks out of the isolation and narcissism of the specialist scholar.' But one has to avoid the other extreme, knowing so much about so many things that nothing can be studied in depth. Thus the necessary balance is between many factors. Too many artists meet uncomprehending criticism during their lives, and die convinced that they are failures.

During his life Cozens (1752–c. 99) remained so unrecognised that he had to earn his living by teaching; yet after his death Constable, in a famous series of lectures on landscape painting, described him as the greatest artist who had ever touched landscape. This delayed recognition is just which should be avoided if possible. Cozens believed that painting which was not naturalistic required instantaneous invention, captured in a first quick sketch at the moment of conception. Watching his students, he thought failure to do so was due to three chief causes: lack of stock ideas laid up in the mind upon which to draw; incapacity to distinguish and connect ideas so treasured up; and want of facility or quickness in execution, causing that first inspiration to fade before the first crude sketch is made. He came across this understanding of the moment of inspiration while wandering among the easels of his students. One student was failing lamentably in his efforts to break with naturalism. Cozens did a quick sketch himself and then saw that some faint marks on his paper had influenced his inventiveness. He was excited by the idea and made faint blots at important spacings on a fresh page. He wanted to write up this idea and looked through what literature he possessed, only to find that Leonardo da Vinci had been there before him, and written in his treatise on painting, 'If you look upon an old wall covered with dirt, or the odd appearance of some streaked stone, you may discover landscapes, uncommon attitudes . . .'

What Rorschach, with his inkblot test, said he had invented around the time of the First World War, had not only been used for experiment in creativity in British laboratories at the turn of the twentieth century. It had been used by Cozens in the eighteenth century, and by Leonardo in the fifteenth and sixteenth centuries. It is unimaginable that Cozens had actually possessed Leonardo's treatise and not read it many times. Yet the moment of truth did not hit him till he was trying to help a failing student. Searching for an explanation of this failure, he brought this fact of creativity sufficiently into consciousness to explain it to students, as well as to use it himself. Constable appreciated Cozens's moment of awareness of the creative conception. So this is why many people are stunned by their first sight of cave paintings. It is a *déjà vu*, I-have-been-here-before experience, ruffling the deepest origins of creativity in numinous excitement. You stand where the artist of so many years ago stood to work with his stone block areas of inspiration. Naturally what came to the cave painter's mind was the great preoccupation with the periodic passing of herds which were his food. We have the same amazement with the paintings of children. They have the genuine moment of creativity to motivate their unskilled pictures.

Just over a century after the death of Cozens, Cézanne was struggling with a new idea and it was one not totally unallied to the fading images upon the retina which Cozens trained his students to catch immediately. Cézanne's great struggle was not so much with his medium as with an idea which would not leave him, and to clarify which he had to straddle the two sides of himself: an almost Blake-like visionary fervour and a compulsive pre-occupation with detail. By temperament he had a very high degree of perseverance. He was as if in the grip of a vice, and when a picture was finished his friends would drag him away to stop him painting any more. In addition to high intelligence, this perseverance which makes one go on and on with a job, and a blazing glory of facility with colour, he had the scientist's patience in studying the minutest detail. A passing artist might have thought, as he stared and stared at a flower, that his subsequent little daub of paint was the best he could do in the way of painting the flower. But he was looking at the background at the same time as the foreground, and the daub was how the two fused to him. He hit on an idea which the psychologists did not discover for another forty years or so. The German psychologist Wertheimer was working on visual perception in his experimental laboratory, and found that the image of what one was watching took a fraction of a second to fade. Out of that discovery there emerged the cinematograph, with photographs of slightly altered positions which gave an illusion of movement. Wertheimer eliminated colour, as nothing to do with this illusion of movement, which he named phi-phenomenon. Whether it was right to eliminate colour completely requires further experimental investi-gation. There is no doubt that many who now have colour television in their homes regard the colour as contributing some-thing more than pretty colours to the picture. It has yet to be proved whether those sensitive to colour do or do not have their awareness of movement heightened by the presence of colour. Such synaethesia, coming together of two forms of senses, such as colour and hearing, known as chromaesthesia, is an established psychological fact for some people.

Cézanne, with his extraordinary sensitivity to colour and the image with its background, became preoccupied with his own experiments in this field. When he had more or less given up outlines, he faintly outlined an onion with the table showing through, or a moving branch with the background also present. He was evidently aware of the as yet unnamed phi-phenomenon. He was aware that he could still see the background as an object moved, or he moved his position against a still life composition. How acute his awareness must have been is demonstrated by the fact that a cinefilm has to use about sixteen frames a second to achieve the illusion of movement. Thus his awareness of the fading image concerned only a fraction of a second. This discovery caused Cézanne to be the first person to equate the background with the foreground in value. He was so excited that he turned from realism to impressionism, to convey what he saw in a glowing assemblage of colour, accents and stress. He knew that he must give supreme attention to natural form. To get the luminous effect that he wanted, he thinned and thinned his oils, till eventually he turned to water colour. This was not because he found water colour harder or easier than oils. It was because water colour was the best medium for the illumination he had had about the background still being visible at the same time as the foreground. Sometimes he needed 100 or 150 sittings to get the final effect; and this while Renoir could catch, for instance, the likeness of Monet's wife, Camille, in a single sitting.

Experiments to catch movement in a static position are as old as culture. Gods were sculptured with, perhaps, half a dozen arms a side, all in different positions, even before the first Egyptian culture. The sculptor of the north door of Chartres Cathedral fashioned God with Adam emerging to one side of him. But the effect of these remains static in a moment of time. Cézanne used the whole panoply of colour, giving his pictures an illusion of movement. By this means he gave movement to foreground and background at the same time. Cézanne's work was rejected by the Paris Salon. At the time of the first Impressionist Exhibition in Paris in 1874, Cézanne was working on 'A Modern Olympus'.

This work was described by one critic as the work of a madman with delirium tremens. Unlike Cozens, Cézanne lived long enough to see the public become a little better informed.

Gainsborough could have worked with this creativity in painting or in music. But he chose to hold a mirror up to society and earn many guineas thereby. However, he found his choice of painting portraits infinitely boring. 'I am sick of portraits,' he told a friend, 'and wish very much to take my *viol-da-gam* and walk off to some sweet village.' Manet rebelled against what society expected of him and said he would paint only what *he* saw. Turner would only paint what had been a primary experience to him. Before he painted 'Snowstorm', now in the National Gallery, he risked his life on the water in a snowstorm to experience what he wanted. Thus we are in Turner's snowstorm when looking at this picture. It is more than a picture. It is a primary experience for us, too. In the same way one goes to the Louvre and experiences the haunting smile of Leonardo's 'Mona Lisa'; or to St Peter's Rome, to see the 'Pietà'. There is an interesting point about the 'Pietà'. One experiences the total exhaustion of Christ but is almost unmoved by the Virgin Mother. Michelangelo did not observe women with the intensity of care that he gave to the observation of men. The mother across whose knees this grown man has collapsed in death is not a living mother; certainly not a mother who is involved in the suffering of her son.

Delacroix was always physically feeble, but his creative energy took him through sixty-five years of achievement. He was a painter with great verbal gifts and he describes how he devoted his life to aesthetics, to what he called 'the good and the beautiful'. Sometimes life proves too overwhelming for a sensitive artist. Anthony Naumann was a poet blinded in the Second World War and did his best to live with this affliction, but committed suicide a quarter of a century later. His uncertainty as to whether he could carry on is seen in this poem :

> Only time can tell
> If in the telling I shall have time for you,
> My gift of living.
> For only time can tell

How the dice will roll;
If you a fool and I a fool,
Breaking every golden rule,
Think everything is under our control . . .

Much of his poetry has this haunting quality.

A few generalisations can be made about the artist and his creative work, which can be gleaned from many sources, such as the above examples. First, the artist has to have primary experiences of such intensity that they rouse a powerful dynamo of feeling. They may re-activate recollections of experience in the first few years, when all children are sensitive enough to experience with the intensity of an artist. Then the artist needs great vigour, which may not be physical but which compels him, as if an urgent message demands communication, and he cannot stop himself. Thirdly, he is drawn to one or more of the various media, such as dance, music, pottery, sculpture, or all the branches of graphic art. Again it is as if he were under compulsion to form the medium in some way. The battle seems to be between the nature of the medium and fashioning it to symbolise this vivid primary experience. Theodorakis used the elusive Greek style of light song to conceal statements which no one was allowed to make; Solzhenitsyn, an unbending giant of literature, wrote with unmistakable truth exactly what happened; Michelangelo crept into the morgue by night to find what lay beneath the surface of men's bodies. This is something the Greeks never did, and even a novice, presented with a Greek statue and one by Michelangelo, could tell which sculptor knew about muscles and bones inside the body. It is said that Leonardo once visited Michelangelo's studio and told him to leave something for his successors to discover.

The fourth generalisation that we can make is that the artist must have immense self-discipline, so that his fight with the medium is successful. For this particular quality he has to have a trait of temperament which the psychologists call perseveration. This really means a tendency to go on doing what you are doing until the task is done. This applies to the creative scientist, too. Kindly people tell them that lunch is ready, that there is a cup of tea waiting, that dinner grows cold, and they seem to fail to register that they have been addressed.

In their way, children have all these characteristics. All of life, even the first nursery rhyme ever heard, is intense primary experience. The feelings roused compel them to express the experience in some medium, be it dance, or song, or making pictures or poetry. Perhaps it is as well that we cannot always catch what they chatter about as they play endlessly with water. That comes from very deep levels, which they repress by about six or seven. They are prepared to try any medium that they find, which can tolerate manipulation. But they do not keep on with one medium for great lengths of time. By four they are making a highly symbolic use of the material: a helmet is a policeman, a veil a bride, adult shoes and a basket together are enough to symbolise a mother at work or at play.

Children are more familiar with the media of art than adults realise. They dance spontaneously if music affects them that way. They make up their own little rhymes and tunes. A boy of four sang in the car:

> I had a little Mummy,
> I had a little Daddy,
> I had a little Scroopy
> And inna popped a hole.

He had perfect pitch and while lying in his pram had been able to reproduce exactly the pitch of the local clock striking. But he became a civil engineer and singing in a choir was an adult hobby. Another boy who could have been artist or craftsman, but became a virologist, was Alan Shattock, son of the Guernsey potters. High above their beautiful pots is a fine abstract painting of a potter bending in relaxed attention over the wheel, made with nothing but thread and nails. This boy showed no notable characteristics at his two secondary schools, first in Surrey and then later at Trinity College, Dublin. Indeed, the teachers said it was a waste of time for him to sit O levels. However, the parents hoped he would become a potter, since the score of pots he had made showed great promise. So they persuaded him, for his own sake to try to get O levels. He not only tried; he succeeded and went on to the university. When it was time to decide what to do, he rejected pottery and chose virology. Then one day, immensely to their surprise, he produced this abstract, an intellectual form of the potter at work. Herbert Read (1931) says the most abstract art of all is found on pottery. It serves no purpose other than beauty. He also says that there is no sculpture that is not preceded by pottery. It is interesting that the boy who was so undistinguished at school and yet was gifted with the artistic and intellectual ability to abstract the essentials of the potter's stance at work, should slip quietly through our educational system almost without notice. We have a long way to go in helping our talented children.

Another boy, son of a musician, was working for his A level music examination and after the excitement of bonfire night celebrations, demonstrated to his father how his mind boggled at the slow improvisation of another boy on the school organ. He showed how he expressed his exasperation by playing his own improvisations at top speed, to his father's intense amusement. During the following March and April he, as part of his examination studies, composed a duet for two pianos. It consisted of a short introduction, a main theme of jazz counterpoint, a slow section, repetition of the main theme and a final coda. It was played at the school concert with an old boy now studying music, and the father's comment was, 'Very professional'. The boy called the duet *Dream Tourist*, presumably feeling that he was touring through his own musical mind. One does not reach this level of creativity in schooldays without considerable support, in this case at school as well as at home.

The teacher who attempts to foster creative talent in normal school circumstances has to be aware of many different arts and prepared to let the children experiment in many different media. But if striking talent is shown, expert help has to be sough⁺ When a school specialises in one of the arts and is in the care of a great exponent, the advantages of sending a talented child there can be great. In 1973 the Yehudi Menuhin School celebrated its tenth anniversary and Mr Menuhin broadcast about his work with the children. In his incomparably sensitive voice he said that he did not know much but there were a few things about which he felt fairly sure. For five centuries Western music had been based on string harmony and we had now reached a critical stage, with very few string players left. He had travelled widely and everywhere he went he found the younger generation thirsting for beauty, for art, to express themselves in the craft. They longed to dedicate themselves to something greater than themselves. He talked of the discipline and the freedom that comes with great performance. He found an enormous potential and latent talent in every child. He founded the school with every teacher of music a performer. Using concepts perennially linked to art discussions, he drew the conclusion that the perilous state of the world today was due to adopting alliances based on supposed advantage and the lie, which could only create distrust. Art, said Mr Menuhin, was here to provide truth and trust.

Anthony Brackenbury, headmaster of the Yehudi Menuhin School, said the children came to the school as a result of an audition, intended to reveal any exceptional musical facility. He doubted if they could really claim more than that. What they were seeking was an eager appetite for music and an obvious love of it. After joining, each child had a Stanford–Binet test with an expert. Results had shown a range of Intelligence Quotient from 93 to 163. To them there seemed to be no connection between the level of intelligence and the musician's ability as a performer. As far as they could tell, musical talent was a relatively separate function. Very acute aural sensibility was quite often, they found, coupled with visual insensitivity. They provided a great deal of musical nourishment for the children. If this was successful, they found there was a surplus of energy and confidence for tackling other matters. However, parental aspirations and anxieties loomed pretty large and the children were under very strong unspoken pressure from home to succeed. Fortunately there was a good market and, unlike actors and dancers, job expectations were good.

In 1973 Mr Menuhin started another scheme, annual concerts for all nations. The idea is that outstanding musicians from every country should give one concert a year for the foundation. 'Music,' says Mr Menuhin, 'is above animosities, and musicians have an

obligation to build as many bridges between nations as they can.'
We have to look to such masterminds as Yehudi Menuhin to give
us such illuminations. There were hard times when he did not
think the school could survive. There may be hard times with the
international scheme, but it is greatly in need of our support and
those who are interested in fostering international understanding
will know that this is a new approach, worthy of support. It has
long been recognised that Western music is an international
language. Orchestras and virtuosos travel extensively, by invitation, playing music from many countries. This new scheme is an
original idea for helping to bridge the damaging gaps between
nations cut off by their differing languages.

When a variety of arts has been examined, it is clear that the
innovator in any medium meets problems over appreciation of a
new art form. It was some time before appreciators could decide
whether impressionists and cubists *and* Picasso, were making fun
of them. Herbert Read, an authority on appreciation and the
meaning of various movements, enabled people to realise that the
impressionists were moving towards the dynamic, as they tried to
see nature through a prism of colour, and the cubists were moving
towards the static, as they analysed and abstracted pure form. The
potter mentioned earlier is a brilliant combination of the two, with
the abstraction of form in a dynamic situation. Those who collect
pictures for financial value have virtually nothing to do with such
appreciation, except as it helps them to know the rubrics by which
they might be able to select pictures which will increase in value.
One of the standard rules for them is that the artist is dead, and
so can produce no fresh original work to devalue what they are
now publicising as the height of a certain artist's work. From the
standpoint of the serious artist, moments of original awareness and
thought have to be recognised and developed. From the standpoint of the serious appreciator, there are two main factors to be
borne in mind. Study is essential to understanding, whether response to a new work is instantaneous or delayed. The second
point is that society goes through periods of consolidating new
forms of art, and periods of breaking up established forms in order
to let through fresh original thinking and awareness.

Keats gives a remarkable account of how he deliberately

distanced himself from events around him, so that he could be anyone or anything, without moral censure concerning ethical values of good and bad. Writing of the poetical character he says:

> . . . it is not itself – it has no self – it is everything and nothing – It has no character – it enjoys light and shade; it lives in gusto, be it foul or fair, high or low, rich or poor, mean or elevated – It has as much delight in conceiving an Iago as an Imogen. What shocks the virtuous philosopher delights the chameleon Poet. It does no harm from its relish of the dark side of things any more than from its taste for the bright one; because they both end in speculation . . . When I am in a room with People, if I ever am free from speculating on creations of my own brain, then not myself goes home to myself: but the identity of everyone in the room begins to press upon me that I am in a little time annihilated – not only among Men; it would be the same in a Nursery of children.
>
> *The Letters of John Keats*, M. Buxton Forman (ed.)

He explained to his fifteen-year-old sister how the virtuous philosophers failed to understand this self-and-not-self game. Then he childed her for telling someone and getting into trouble. He reminded her of the sort of people children have to associate with, meaning, presumably, uncomprehending adults. In the light of Keats' practised aesthetic distance, it is interesting to note that he thought Shakespeare became too involved in writing *King Lear* to the detriment of the play.

A committee of the World Organisation for Early Childhood Education (OMEP) met in Unesco House, Paris, just after Picasso's mural there was completed. Many who came to look went away in disgust at the new Picasso joke. Maybe Picasso wished appreciators to play the self-and-not-self game in viewing it. To one viewer at least, it seemed to be a double skit on Rubens and the puritanical tradition. There was a huge party of lounging figures in vivid colour, and plummetting down headfirst into the abyss there was a thin silhouette in black of a puritanical figure. Many people were so shocked by the monstrous party that they failed to notice the black figure plunging to its doom. Herbert Read points out, in his *The Meaning of Art*, that after the art has been studied, there is the psychological aspect to contend with. It may be that Picasso hoped to shock people into seeing the lethal dichotomy of a society which could not span the two, the decadent and the noble. It could well have been one of Picasso's greatest efforts towards society's integrity. But it has now been removed.

Thinking of Picasso turns one's thought back to the children, whose spontaneous creativity seemed to infiltrate so much of his work. It is clear that young children, within the limits of their development, are *bona fide* artists. They can avail themselves of any medium, untrammelled by ideas of what society expects of them. All that adults need to do at first is to give them opportunity in the whole wide spectrum of art and then foster those arts they enjoy most as they grow older. When they become adult, if they are without art as hobby or profession, this is an immeasurable loss to their struggle towards integrity of personality. Who shall decide where the talents of individual children lie? It cannot be just left to the children, as most lose courage in early adolescence. It cannot be left to parents, because they are only rarely experts in any of the arts. Moreover, there is the danger of parents putting too much pressure on the children to succeed in an art. During the Second World War a brilliant violinist of seven was brought to the child guidance clinic of a London teaching hospital because he had gone on strike and would not so much as touch the violin. When the psychiatrist had established good rapport, he asked why he had ever taken up the violin. The child put his finger on the exact spot for diagnosis, when he said, 'It was my mother's ambition.'

We are so ignorant about the talents of children that we have adopted a most unscientific procedure and, arguing by analogy, assumed that there will be about the same distribution of artistic talent as of intelligence: that is to say, about 2 to 3 per cent of children with exceptional talents. The Americans, who are doing high-level research here, think that the number of children with special talents is nearer 10 to 12 per cent. This is not really surprising, since we now know that all children are genuine artists to some degree. We also know that for countless centuries civilisations have risen and collapsed, because over and over again they have failed to span the decadent and the noble, as for instance presented in pictorial form by Picasso in Unesco House, in the disaster phase. We have to consider, as one possible hypothesis, the damaging effect upon integrity of personality, not merely in suppressing, but far worse – despising art as a useless, non-profit-making occupation.

The cave painters did not have this contempt for art. They knew some mastery was attained by it, and used the pictures for ritual magic. Before the paintings on the wall, they would have used outlines on the ground, still used today, as areas in which before hunting they got themselves in trim with preliminary shots. They then trusted themselves to the gods. Succeeding religions, including the Christian one, did not have such contempt. Their places of worship have always included such arts as music, painting and movement. From this art, people could emerge trusting to the gods or to one God. It was Abraham who made the mighty integrative abstraction of there being only one single God, and left Ur with a small band who could understand what he meant. Now today many people have abandoned the idea of there being one eminent force far exceeding their comprehension. Disastrously, many of these have lost their way in supplanting this concept with egotism alone, forgetting that man is by nature also altruistic. This is not so with great humanists, such as Claude Montefiore, whose work in education has already been referred to in Chapter 2.

Where should one turn now to understand how to foster integrity through art, and specifically with children of exceptional ability? Four specialists in working with talented children have been kind enough to give their opinions about such children in four different areas of art. They are, in order of presentation:

Bernard Ollis, Dip. A., a student at the Royal College of Art recommended by his professor, who has worked with children.

Muriel Judd, LRAM, Dip. Drama and Art, who has worked for many years in Speech and Drama, with students and children, at the Maria Grey College of Education. She is on the Panel of Advisers of the NAGC.

Arnold Haskell, CBE, D. Litt, for twenty years Director of the Royal Ballet School.

Michal Hambourg, concert pianist and teacher of pianoforte. Her mother was a violinist of professional level and her father the world-famous concert pianist Mark Hambourg. She is on the Panel of Advisers of the NAGC.

None of them saw this chapter before being asked to express their views on children of talent. There could be no better conclusion to this chapter than to ask them to speak.

BERNARD OLLIS

The question of detecting and fostering talent in painting and other graphic arts is, I find, a very complex one. In terms of aesthetic value, rights and wrongs are difficult to assess. However, there are of course general guidelines in the stages of development. 'The child sees the world differently from the way he draws and paints it' (Lowenfield, *Creative and Mental Growth*). In consequence any interference from outside, from either teacher or parent, changes the child's intuitive expression. Through misunderstanding, it is very easy for the adult to create the notion of 'realistic' drawing, and the child being 'good' or 'bad' in comparison with how the adult sees reality. The child's concerns are with his own emphasis, exaggerations and realities, which differ immensely from physical sizes. To comment on the talented child, it is necessary to go through the basic stages.

From about two years onwards, the child's preoccupation is with a mark-making, that can only be described as uncontrolled scribbling. This normal activity of scribbling, this freedom from which a young child derives so much pleasure, can all too easily be stifled by adult criticism and failure to understand.

Slightly later, the child shows that he is learning to develop control, in the form of marks and lines which he repeats in some fashion. This tells us that he has learnt to reproduce. These first signs of controlled behaviour connect strongly with the child's learning to repeat words to express himself.

These experiences gain ground when they are linked with storytelling, which the child spontaneously wants to illustrate.

However, the physical lines in no way summarise or depict the physical form realistically. This state of powerful expression is one that cannot be recaptured in the same spirit by adults, since the knowledge learnt inhibits and conditions this act, till the picture becomes completely contrived. The child moves ahead towards basic symbols, e.g. circles which may represent head, wheel, etc., and longitudinal lines, which are often equivalents for the lines of the body. This activity, now for the first time recognised by the adult, often results in stronger contact and encouragement in the direction of visual self-expression.

I often find it strange that two dots, a triangle and a line inside a circle, cannot only convey 'face' to the observer but often the mood of expression of the face.

Of course the child is flexible and spontaneous, but also vulnerable. It is therefore important that the teacher helps rather than hinders, and shows enthusiasm over the basic, but very complex, mark-making.

All through this period the space is flat and colour is used primarily for pleasure and reinforcement of shape. Size is not related to perspective, but to importance; and spatial techniques, like blue for the background and red for the foreground, are not consciously thought out. The whole creation, however, is so real in essence, so simplified, direct and intuitive, that I find it exciting in nearly all normal young children. In consequence, I suppose that what stimulates me to express a greater appreciation of one rather than another is originality of design – an overall feel – a complete spontaneous action that seems unhindered in appearance.

A child often has problems in negotiating certain objects or subject-matters; and in consequence, when the child is in control of the language I can appreciate the picture more readily. Often again, the child tries to imitate, maybe copying his elder brothers or sisters, and this often leads to problems. An imitated piece of work usually looks tentative and prolonged, as what was a spontaneous stroke in the original has to be carefully copied. The child's work under normal conditions still possesses this freedom of line and movement. Objects often look as if they are floating in space, rather than on one base line. But at a still later stage more sophisticated techniques come into play, such as overlapping of objects, and figures drawn from life rather than the child's own imagination. This in turn causes a new realism, which takes the child into boundless areas of creativity. Attempts to measure and test at this stage are very dubious.

You can only relate one age group to another and find a child who has in fact reached a stage before his age group normally would, or in the same way find a child who has failed to attain what is normal for his age. Some think it possible to set up tests along such lines of group developmental comparisons and grade ability through these comparisons. This has been tried by many American psychologists but results have repeatedly shown that they were not tests of creative talent, but only of intelligence. In my opinion the failure is in the basic assumption. You cannot expect a child to perform at a given moment, in a given place, along with others in the test situation. It is the very freedom of choice, in time and situation, which leads to the most original and powerful expressions.

However, it is quite possible to see a critical awareness, an objective analysis by a child regarding his own work, long before older children, even before most adolescents, have this capability. In extreme cases the child may be rated a genius of his age. However, critical awareness does not stop at any one stage. It develops continuously into adulthood and is increasingly enriched by maturity.

Too often in the adolescent stage interest wanes. The person is influenced by notions of 'good' and 'bad' in relation to his own realism of drawing or painting. In this misdirected awareness he loses confidence and turns to other forms of self-expression. Also, he may never again so spontaneously use visual perception as a source of creativity.

If the person does continue, and he does have the capacity to draw or paint accurately from life, he still needs to pause and ask himself questions. It is not everything just to have a very sophisticated technique, or to be a skilled craftsman. Ideas and imagination still need to be understood and acted upon.

The artist may have an intellectual attitude towards himself and his environment or he may experience some social message which he needs to put forward. Or it may be that he has an extreme, but natural and intuitive, feel for paint or other materials. Whatever his motivation, he has to work through his personal feelings in such a way that his work of art evokes sympathetic emotion in the onlooker. The field is infinite. The work demands of the artist both dedication and hard work.

MURIEL JUDD

'I think it happened when I came to love Shakespeare at school . . . we were encouraged to *act* Shakespeare, not just to study him.' This was Dame Peggy Ashcroft's reply to a query during a television interview which asked her what was her first impulse towards acting.

It is possibly more difficult than in other arts to identify the child who has the potential to make his future career in the theatre. This assessment is bound to be subjective. Success in the theatre is dependent on so many factors. Children with star quality rarely continue in the profession into adult life and many who show talent at school develop quite different skills with maturity and may become doctors, lawyers or scientists, retaining only secondary interest in dramatic affairs.

It is essential to understand the difference between the aims of drama in education and those involved in theatre training. Both may be concerned with interpretation of dramatic literature or the themes involved in a dramatic conflict. But in a theatrical performance, the actor is trained to transmit his interpretation to an audience; and in education, his work in drama is leading the child towards self-discovery.

The actor must learn to discipline his body, his voice, his movement and his emotions through long and exhausting training and rehearsals. It is unwise to engage in this while a child is still growing physically and mentally. As with a singer, some maturity must have been reached before exacting training can commence.

'When I was a child, I spake as a child, I understood as a child, I thought as a child: but when I became a man, I put away childish things.'[1]

[1] *The Bible*, authorised version: 1 Cor. 13: 11.

An actor is an intermediary between the dramatist and the audience. Through him the audience sees the dramatist's ideas conveyed in terms of theatre. The actor may also be controlled by the wishes of the director and to some extent have to subdue his own interpretation. He will be presenting his performance in an artificial situation, surrounded by the mechanism and trappings of stage setting, lighting and costume.

An amateur actor may find this a very enjoyable experience, whether an adult or a child. Many talented children will relish the opportunity to extend themselves and their energies in the hustle and bustle of 'putting on a play'. The professional actor will always find this a hard job, in which only those with physical stamina and determination, and perhaps good luck as well as talent, will attain even moderate success.

Drama in education is not concerned with preparing children for this hazardous future. Those who have star quality will find their own way to the theatre, whether they start as milliners, as did Dame Edith Evans, or office clerks, as did Sir Ralph Richardson. The aim of drama in education is to deepen the total learning experience. It should involve a child physically, mentally and emotionally in learning more about himself, his place in the world and his relationship with others.

All young children use dramatic play to resolve some of their problems. In school they will be helped, through improvised drama and by role-playing, to meet the demands that increased social awareness will bring. They will be prepared to find in their improvised drama and in the plays which they study, a deeper appreciation of how a dramatist can present the conflict of character and situation, and how these problems may be faced if not solved. Such personal discovery does not require an audience or the external effects associated with the theatre. It requires a sympathetic teacher and room to move and make a noise. The able child is well equipped to savour the effect of the sounds of poetry and fine prose if he is given the opportunity to get on his feet and say the words.

'Originally Shakespeare excited me because of the words, but then it became the excitement of character and drama; the fascination of a character living apart from you becoming that character, or involving yourself in it; finding out how to make the character alive.'[1]

The gifted child will bring his own particular characteristics and qualities to this work. He may have in abundance those very qualities which a teacher is seeking to induce through dramatic activity. The child may not be an outstanding actor; but because he can absorb information rapidly, make quick observations and deductions from his experience, he will draw on these for his improvised drama. The dramatic experience will deepen his own awareness of his place in the world.

A child's use of language reflects his wide-ranging thinking. He may have a sensitive ear and show ability to imitate conversations and mannerisms of talking which he has chanced to hear. He will want to talk and share his ideas with adults and his peers. With younger children, dramatic play provides an opportunity for language to develop; older children will draw from their own reading of books, plays and poems in their conversation and in role-playing.

Gifted children are usually prolific readers and for a child who has a chance and interest to enjoy drama in school, reading will open up ever-widening vistas for his imagination and an opportunity to play out his wildest fantasies.

Following a visit to 'The Treasures of Tutankhamen', a group of children organised their own discovery, led by a very gifted little girl of seven. They created their own artefacts of an imagined civilisation, disguised themselves as mummies and arranged to be found! The making of the mysterious properties and the working out of how they might be discovered by archaeologists occupied many more hours of research than the actual dramatic episode.

Drama in school is not concerned with simply playing out stories but with helping children to see the significance of the relationships between people, the choice and decision which must be made by the hero, the problems which must be solved. It is from the close association with literature and with real-life experience that children will be able to cope with the problems of their own lives. Classroom drama will give an opportunity for the development of

[1] Peggy Ashcroft to David Jones, *Great Acting*, Hal Burton (ed.).

social awareness. It will help a child to find satisfaction from a variety of roles, not necessarily that of the leader or hero. A gifted child may be isolated from his peers in some areas of work by reason of his ability; in drama he can choose and can learn to take a less dominant role. The skilled teacher knows that personal exhibition is unlikely to have more than superficial success.

There will always be those children who, because of their physical appearance or attractiveness of voice and movement, may have professional success in the theatre, the film industry or on television. These children may be exploited for commercial reasons by parents or stage schools. Many are undoubtedly talented, intelligent children and, if sensitively trained and managed, will enjoy the experience of fame and spotlight. It does seem, however, that a large number of child stars burn out before maturity.

The gifted child will develop a range of talents during his early years in school. He will be 'good' at many pursuits, artistic, scientific and athletic. If he is given the chance through a liberal education to extend his creativity, his work in drama should ensure confidence and freedom of verbal expression, a delight in language and in poetry, and a deeper sensitivity to his fellow human beings. He will then find his own path to a future career.

ARNOLD HASKELL

The assessment of talent in the young dancer, and this would to a degree apply to the athlete, is different and in many ways more difficult than in the case of the artistic child in general.

We are looking for two separate things: physical aptitude and artistic ability. We must remember that the dancer is both the instrument and the instrumentalist. The perfect instrument scarcely exists but skilled training, which is rare, can, within limits, overcome certain physical disabilities. The dancer, if intelligent enough, can often turn a fault into a virtue. I use the word intelligent because it is essential in an art that requires very rapid reflexes, a knowledge of style and a good memory. In my experience I have never known pupils with a low IQ do well in ballet, however excellent a start they may make. The dancer may not necessarily have an academic mind, though in very many cases success in ballet-training goes hand in hand with success in school-work.

It is important to stress one point. This is a risky career, because there is great competition and up to the last moment in training there can be mishaps, sudden rapid growth, and so on. Such insecurity is obviously not ideal for any child. Those who handle dance pupils must therefore never be lavish in praise. The attitude is always one of 'so far, so good'. The dancer, fortunately, is essentially a realist, though in too many cases the parents are not. The work itself is a training in realism. The audience is conscious of the glamour. The dancer knows only too well how she has performed.

I can remember Pavlova telling me after a rapturous reception, 'I wish they had not applauded so much. I know I did not dance so well tonight. It is essential to keep up standards.'

I have not discussed the artist yet. The word artist is much abused. The vast majority of dancers in a good company are fine craftsmen, and that is a noble word. In addition to craftsmanship the dancer needs musicality, the power to convey emotion with the whole body, in fact a touch of that magic that is at the origin of all the arts. No training can provide that, but faulty training can destroy it.

The great teacher of dancing is as rare as the ballerina and though the dance teacher must have had considerable stage experience she need not have been an outstanding dancer herself. On the contrary the better teacher is often one who has realised her shortcomings.

Agrippina Vaganova, the greatest teacher of the twentieth century, was a ballerina but not of great distinction. She could analyse, communicate and create, giving to her dancers a hallmark that was unmistakable.

MICHAL HAMBOURG

To a musician who has music as the key to his creative being from the beginning, music is a must, a vision. A baby of three to four months responds to rhythm, one of the basic elements of life. Those to whom music is important and who have true musicality cannot stand very loud sounds, perpetual noise, or background sound. When innately musical children reach the age of three years they love to dance and sing, and try to play an instrument. These activities should be encouraged but not pushed. In the early development of creativity the artist is born, and his first awareness of music must be a private exploring experience. Opportunities to help him discover music must be there but it is nurturing, with affection and sympathy, that is required. Often, because parents are ambitious and anxious, they inhibit that which is creative in a gifted musical child by structured teaching too soon.

Around five years old it is essential to find a sympathetic and enlightened teacher who specialises in young children. At this stage children's hands and muscles are still very small and delicate, and they must start to play with the minimum amount of tension; everything should take place in a very informal relaxed way. At this age children are very serious in wanting to learn, and if the teacher is too exacting the child may never express his own ideas and will try to copy the teacher in order to conform. The ultimate result of this will be a proficient technician who has lost the art of interpretation because individuality has been inhibited. I feel it is important to have a small panel of experienced musicians for parents of musical children to consult, who will advise on the best ways of developing talent.

Musical people hear music all the time when doing other things; as I write this, I hear a phrase of Schubert which I have been thinking about for some days. In musical children this pre-occupation is often misunderstood for lack of attention; but it is really a creative process and must be understood as such.

The true musician will not be able to keep away from his instrument, and he may need to experiment before he finds the one that is really for him; it is said that people should always start by learning the piano, but I don't hold with this unless a child feels drawn to the instrument; there are many ways of beginning to learn music, by playing recorders, singing, etc. What is essential is the opportunity to listen and get to know all kinds of music; musical children need musical libraries. Pianists need works of Beethoven, Mozart, Bach, standard classics to read and explore. If a child is truly talented, he will read music very easily, once he has assimilated the notation; it is often easier for him to read music, which has immediate meaning for him, than words. I remember when I was about eight years old reading the preludes and fugues and inventions of Bach, trying the early sonatas of Beethoven, playing anything I could find. This was my 'fun', quite separate from the daily practice which is the beginning of musical discipline, and needs careful help. Children of seven to eight should not work at this for more than one hour daily, divided into two periods; this work is learning a discipline, learning concentration in playing, and great care should be taken in avoiding fatigue. Another necessity is time for quiet, an essential part of becoming a musician, a quiet place where you can concentrate on musical ideas or listen to records, and think undisturbed. This is a basic part of the musician's way of life and many artists are lost when the family does not understand and provide this ambience.

When children grow older, they are often taken to concerts. Under the age of eleven they should not be expected to sit through a whole concert, however much they think they can. In musical children the quality and concentration of listening is different from that of the average listener, and they become either exhausted or overstimulated by too much listening. For them music is not a drug, and it must remain full of meaning. To young people who are musically sensitive the powerful sounds of an orchestra can be unbearably painful; also music is the point of immense feeling in their lives and sometimes they find that they cannot endure the things that music says to them. I remember particularly a small girl of five who simply could not listen and burst into tears because she said the music made her feel so terribly sad. At such times one must comfort by explaining that music means many different and deeply moving things, and that these feelings are experienced by all musicians as they begin to understand music.

Good teachers are worth their weight in gold; they have to protect and guide their pupils through many problems, psychological, musical and practical; and they have to advise and help parents, dissuading them from letting their children play in public until they are ready to cope with the nervous strain, and even then carefully spacing the concerts. When a musician is under stress he cannot 'play out his feelings' in music as this is a negation of interpretation; the therapy is to be helped to find your way back to the meaning of the composer's idea, to the return of musical integrity through the instrument or manuscript, and the revival of creative activity. Often children write down musical sounds that come into their heads; sometimes these are disconnected phrases, musical but strange. This music often comes into the mind as you fall asleep or wake. The moment of waking when young, and in your true centre, is a marvellous experience, over-flowing with happiness. When I awoke in the country and rushed out, it was like being a part of a great work of music. When I think back to my childhood I always think of a world filled with sound; in our home music was played all day and a large part of the night. Gradually as I grew older, about twelve, I began to learn the true disciplines of the work. At this time careful work disciplines must be planned. Musicians need to adjust to their own work schedule, usually a very tight one, as schoolwork must be fitted around practice periods, and time must be made for relaxa-tion and rest periods.

A very real method of communication is to talk with other people who know and love music. The great pleasure is to know that they too hear and experience music as you do; differences can be explained in terms of sound which might take years to explain through words alone. In music I think the composer has the hardest role; others have to interpret for him and yet others listen. I sometimes think he should be allowed to compose the audience! The interpreter is a bridge between the composer and the listener, a role of great responsibility which young musicians must be helped to understand from the beginning: firstly by sup-porting and fostering their confidence in their musical being, then gradually introducing the realisation of their responsibility in the use of their talents; encouraging them to think musically and to listen to their phrasing as they play; this is a form of intense con-centration which artists spend their lives perfecting.

In adolescence a whole new set of problems occur, centred on an extending range of emotions and feelings. Very young people won't suffer from nerves and anxieties when playing to audiences;

most of them love performing and showing what they can do. Almost overnight, around the age of thirteen, they start to be nervous and it is as if a new awareness is thrust upon them. At this time children should not be pushed into concert playing. They need and want to say more and to say it better. They are becoming aware of a very much deeper approach to musical life; something in them realises that there is a far wider musical spectrum before them, and that they are going to interpret a whole world of ideas and emotions in music which, as yet, they do not know.

At this time young people become very self-conscious about their appearance and how they look on the platform. I remember feeling desperate when I was thirteen and going to play Saint-Saëns' concerto in G minor. I can still remember every moment of this unutterable experience. I had to go on stage dressed in orange, in a garment which my mother thought too lovely for words, with little frills from top to bottom, *which I despised*! I remember the feeling of rage with which I lumbered on to the platform. But luckily, as always happens, when I sat down to play, the whole thing was so marvellous and so consuming that I forgot about my orange-like appearance. By the end it did not matter anyhow. Other people have told me of the same sort of experience when appearing before the public in adolescence.

Provided that there is love and encouragement, young musicians really love to work and learn; a tremendous amount of study and dedication is necessary; when other people are listening, it adds a new dimension, and therefore it is important to play to friends and family; but public performance is something different and a great strain; so during the adolescent years of study and preparation it must be kept to a minimum. In order to relate to music as an art, the pupil in his teens must learn to understand the whole idea of art in a much wider context; this involves many different studies, and a true appraisal of your function as a performer, a small but indispensable piece of this vast canvas.

This is why it is so important to find out the potential of those musical children who need help and advice. Some will not need this wide and comprehensive musical education; those who are not going to become professional musicians can learn some techniques and have fun making music. But serious musicians in their early teens should spend around four hours a day working in music, as well as listening to records and playing for pleasure. I should say here that different instruments require different disciplines, and it is the good teacher who plans and advises on the pupil's schedule.

5

THE PARENTS AND THEIR CHILDREN

During the very early days of the National Association for Gifted Children, of which I was a founder member, all who were elected chairmen of branches had extremely large areas to look after. Mine stretched from Kent, along the south of London, to Surrey and Sussex, Hampshire, Berkshire, and included Buckinghamshire as well. With some persuasion all but Surrey became autonomous, and I was left chairman of Surrey. Because of this initial large area, children were brought long distances for me to assess them, in case their difficulties might be due to exceptional gifts or talents. If they proved exceptional I charged five guineas instead of seven, provided they joined the NAGC. The fee was to remind people that assessment of intelligence was a skilled job; and the reduction for members was to help headquarters gain new members.

Of the children to whom I gave the 1960 revision of the Stanford–Binet Intelligence Scale, fifty-five proved to have Intelligence Quotients over 130 and one other child, as explained later, had brilliant mathematical ability but was so alarmed by what she took to be a school situation that no fair assessment was possible. Incidentally, she made a complete fool of me for testing her with one-inch cubes when she was accustomed to a slide rule. Another boy of four insisted, with a most engaging smile, that he could only think while standing on his head. I was convinced that his IQ was over 145, so I offered to re-test him free in a couple of years. When he returned the results proved to be IQ 167. Another boy with exceptional talent was re-tested, after I had left Surrey, by a colleague, and the change from a withdrawn boy who had no use for contemporaries to a lively fellow making his contribution to society also resulted in apparent rise of IQ. This last point, apparent rise of IQ, suggests a valuable area of research. Gifted and talented children who are removed from unsuitable environments to favourable ones should be re-assessed after a couple of years, to find out whether there is statistically significant evidence of the improvement of functioning of intelligence under these new circumstances. This should, of course, be done for all children; but here we are specifically considering gifted children.

Table 6 INTELLIGENCE QUOTIENTS OF FIFTY-FIVE GIFTED CHILDREN[1]

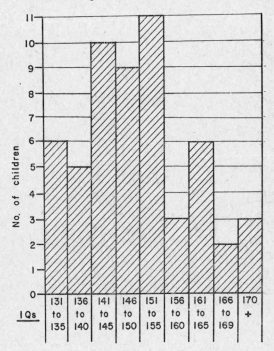

Table 6 is a graph of the fifty-five IQs obtained. Letters were sent to all of the parents asking how these children were now getting on, both in and out of school. Of the parents who were kind enough to reply, most of them were extremely glad to explain the position now. Judging by what the parents said, those with IQ 131 to 140 were reasonably happy in school if they had a

[1] *Assessed by P. M. Pickard by Stanford-Binet Scale (1960 revision) 1966–72.*

sympathetic teacher. Those with IQ in the 140s were not doing so well, unless the teacher took an active interest in gifted children and had made a study of how to help them. But almost nobody was happy in a normal school with IQ over 150. As will appear shortly, a number of parents had found sympathetic public schools, run on progressive lines, which were flexible enough to help even those with IQ above 160. There, a tutorial system and a very wide range of possible studies enabled these children to work at their own pace in their own ways. But one or two nearly lost the chance through not learning how to study in State junior schools.

The circumstances in which I was able to observe these children were most fortunate. They came to me, at their request, and my house was on a Surrey hill. The garden had a one-in-eight fall and there were three shelves of lawn. There was a garden trolley on which the children rode down, avoiding trees, shrubs, vegetable and flower-beds; and when they wished to stop they steered the trolley round to try to go uphill. I gave the Stanford–Binet test in the house. When I wanted to talk to the parents I could also watch the children, and see their varying reactions on the trolley, which each one thoroughly enjoyed. My husband was an electronics inventor with a laboratory in the garden. As we had a copper roof, he could also show the slot aerials which he had invented during the Second World War. We tried to arrange these meetings at the weekend, as he so enjoyed answering the children's questions.

This chapter is not in the ordinary sense based on research. When I showed the above graph to Professor Burt, he asked how I had found them. I did not. They found me. So for a start, there was no 'correct selection technique'. Over the years I had long discussions with the parents on these visits and in our committee meetings. I wrote to every one of the parents whose child is represented in this graph, as well as a very few others with gifted children who had not been assessed by me, asking if they would tell me anything they liked for this book about their gifted children. I explained that I was trying to throw some fresh light on having a gifted and/or talented child in the family; and also trying to help those who might be planning high-level research on gifted and talented children. Some parents had moved away; some doubtless meant to answer and never got down to it; one or two answered so late that I was still altering this chapter when it had to go to press. In all, twenty-seven families replied. When the chapter was in its almost final form, every parent of a child mentioned in the rest of this chapter saw the draft and any requested additions or subtractions were made. What follows is not a series of child studies but a series of characteristics of gifted and talented children as revealed by the children and in conversation and correspondence between me and their parents.

First, it is interesting to see whether the individual potential of these children was developing in ways which enabled them to achieve success, in school or anywhere else. One girl, now fifteen and at a progressive public school, has decided to go to Oxford or Cambridge (she does not mind which), in order to become a barrister. Her father is an OBE; and her mother, a qualified teacher, says trenchantly, 'She will be whatever she wants to be.' Another mother who is a teacher reports that one daughter got ten O levels at fifteen, four of which were A grades: French, Latin, Geography and Mathematics, with French a double A. Another mother said her son had won a scholarship to Manchester Grammar School, coming fourth of all entrants. They did not take this up as it involved a long daily journey. But he went to another public school (founded in 1524), which was nearer his home. Another one said her daughter of exceptionally high ability struck a very unhappy patch in her progressive public school, through a most vindictive master. It takes time to get rid of a bad master, but the head was well aware of what was happening and got round the trouble by giving the girl a scholarship to the senior school. She was suddenly transformed from a failure to being as happy as her friends. It is important to mention that she is in the highest column of this graph, with IQ 170+, as one of the problems for gifted children is the jealousy they arouse. Family rejoicing was great, but the mother said she was a wiser girl for learning what antagonism brightness can arouse. Her sister, with IQ in the top half of the 140s, was doing well at the same school, particularly in music.

There are four more children whose progress should be noted.

Two brothers were doing well in the lower school of a progressive public school and there was some doubt as to what would happen when the older one went up to the senior school. He has now gone up and the masters still praise him for both keenness and independence.

An incident concerning their sleep patterns is worth describing. We told all parents not to worry if their children needed less sleep than most children, but to put suitable toys for the night, so that they could leave their parents in peace. So the bedrooms of these two brothers were well equipped by a mother who had been trained as a teacher. But their sleeping patterns were not the same. First one would wake for a couple of hours and then the other, with some four hours of the night devoted to Brumm-brumm and other strange noises. 'We feel,' said the parents laughing, 'as if we are living over Waterloo Station.'

These brothers are strong and vital people. Their mother commented how lucky they were to have had no problems. Perhaps it would be more accurate to say how lucky the boys were to have parents who understood their requirements. The older boy had a tape-recorder and electronic material, much of it salvaged from old television sets. He would invent his own experiments and tape-record his ideas as they came to him in the night. The mother's father always said his best ideas came to him in the night. This is also reported by many distinguished artists and scientists. When the younger one woke he would pace up and down telling himself about a race of people called the Dumpers, founded by the original Dumper and Dumpa-Lala. There was even a Dumper Solar System which he was able to draw and explain in such detail as what gases surrounded each planet. One planet was called Mowfitamine. So many different voices were used in the recounting of this serial that his father used to say he thought thieves must have broken into the house. When the older brother was twelve, the mowing machine was said to be beyond repair. He took it completely to pieces, stripped the machine, cleaning and oiling every part and repairing with rust-protecting paint where necessary. It worked again. So the boys drew up plans for a holiday business partnership for mower maintenance, in order to augment pocket money.

The other two who should be mentioned for their achievement are also boys, but not related. They are both musical. The first came to me when he was seven and played five simple pieces of Bach from memory on the piano, with great precision. Through the NAGC he got into the Yehudi Menuhin School, and as it was in Surrey, we often went over to hear their concerts. His father was on the Surrey committee and we had long discussions as to what should happen if he proved not sufficiently talented musically to earn his living that way. Finally we decided that it would be better for him to have a few years of drenching himself in music, even if he had to go to a technical college afterwards to get some quite different paper qualification. We need not have worried. He won a music scholarship to the most famous school in the world. His father's description of him after the first few months captures his happiness there: 'They really do things on a grand scale there and he finds himself involved with orchestra work, choir, ensembles and madrigals, quite apart from his piano studies – so I think his feet have not yet touched the ground.' At first it was a half scholarship that he won, but after a probationary term it became a full scholarship, which was indeed something for the parents to be proud of. This boy was also a member of the National Youth Orchestra, so holidays were partly taken up with courses. They were televised for the Albert Hall and he was mentioned as the youngest. However, his section was not actually shown and he was healthily indignant about this.

The other musical boy came to me when he was six. He had been told that he could have violin lessons when he was six. But he had found a violin when he was barely five, set it up and taught himself to play. So his parents gave in and he started lessons at five. He had been playing for a year when he came to me to be assessed. His intelligence, as well as his musical ability, was outstanding. His older sister, about eight, had come too, for the family outing. My husband got down a large German book of prehistoric monsters. *She* took *him* through the book naming every species and giving many details, though she knew no German. We were accustomed to being astonished ourselves but not to the parents being astonished. Both parents said they had no idea where she had got the information. Two or three times she laughed merrily and said she had read about this one but never seen a picture of it before.

That this was an extremely close and happy family was made very clear all through the visit. At the last moment the boy went across the room to look at something and the girl started to tell me something in a low, quick voice. The parents came near to share the story. She said that a week or two ago all four had gone to a 'cello recital. They were looking forward to the boy's reaction to his first experience of a 'cello. She said that his face was astounding. The faces of the sister and parents became blank and open-mouthed to show his utter amazement. It was, they said, some minutes before the boy became lost in the music, as he had never dreamed that it might be possible to hold a violin upside down. When the concert was over he would not allow them to dally. He insisted that they went home immediately. Once there he went straight to the cupboard where his violin was kept. Not stopping to tune it or get himself a chair, he did a gymnastic knees-outward-bend, inverted his violin between his knees, and immediately played a perfectly adequate and recognisable tune. The parents are now giving him twenty-five minutes daily violin practice, one or other accompanying him.

From these incidents it is clear that some of the children in this group are achieving success. True, the last incident of the little violinist was success outside school, within the home. But it was closely related to what could have happened in school, because the father is a music teacher. Obviously, here is one teacher not opposed to gifted or talented children – and we still count them in ones. We will return to this violinist in connection with boredom in school.

Parents had some very penetrating remarks to make about emotionality. The girl who plans Oxbridge as the route to becoming a barrister makes friends easily but has a quick temper and 'is her own worst enemy', in that she often makes very sarcastic remarks. The two young boys with different sleeping patterns might have passed as without anxiety but for a very perceptive mother. Each had shown a certain watchfulness on first going to school, which was allayed on finding he could manage well; and again, on the older one going to the upper school, each felt the anxiety of new situations, but once more they found they could manage without each other. They are both such forceful characters that this parental perceptiveness must have eased the situations for them. Their vitality could have been mistaken for confidence.

One girl came who was four years ten months, but it proved impossible to give a mental age, so she has had to be left off the graph in Table 6. Her anxiety caused her to cling to her own books and talk almost entirely about them. Both parents are engineers and I finally caught her attention with a problem of one-inch cubes. This comes at the six-year level and seemed a promising start. However, as I asked her to put on to a piece of paper first one number of cubes then another, and again another, she did it correctly but gave me an extremely odd look each time. It was only afterwards that I found she was accustomed to using a slide rule at home. Soon after this she changed to a very understanding school and now, according to the mother, she plays easily and works hard.

Here again, there might have been severe problems if the parents had not been able to learn from their daughter how her life should be run. She is now seven. There is an unusual rhythm of living which she has herself evolved, and which the parents can accept. She has a session of a few weeks when she works on academic subjects and other interests almost non-stop for all the hours she can keep awake. Then suddenly she will switch off and appear almost dumb about perfectly easy things. Next comes a great eating session when they cannot find enough to feed her. This seems to be a stoking-up session, ready for the next work session, which follows. They have noticed this over and over again. She has to leave her present school now she is seven. But there appears to be no understanding from local educationists. So the father is changing his job, so that they can move near a good day school. This is just as well as their son, now four, is her able assistant at experiments, and has already informed himself well on reading, arithmetic and history. His bed-time reading is Roman Britain, Julius Caesar, Alexander the Great, and so on, all ably set forth in Ladybird books.

All but one of these nine children, about whom it was specifically stated that they had won through to academic success, were at progressive public schools, where children were seen as individuals. The ninth child attended an ancient local grammar school. Several parents mentioned how right it seemed for their children to be with others of similar ability, because it gave them a chance to feel normal themselves. We are in urgent need of research to find out whether we have any right to expect normal or even comprehensive schools to be sufficiently flexible to accommodate children of IQ over 160. It is no solution to move a child up more than a couple of years, as this is damaging to social development. In my work with gifted children, I found that much could be done by two adaptations: first, at least an hour of private study each day, when an absorbed class did not notice at what level any other child was studying; and then by contributions to sociability of a complexity not observed by others, such as editing a newspaper, producing a play, drawing up sports lists, and so on. But we have to train teachers to sufficient flexibility and knowledge of advanced programmes to carry out such administration in a class.

Some parents specifically mentioned emotional aspects. Some were not too much in trouble, but others had severe difficulties. The father of the boy who won a music scholarship to a public school describes how his son is emerging from what has been quite serious withdrawal from contemporaries. He has differing responses to other children and to other adults, neither yet quite stable. With children of his own age but less ability, he adapts his conversational level with ease but becomes argumentative, even when quite ignorant of the subject. He is not yet really sociable with them, but requires them for table games, for cards, and so on. But he really enjoys adult company and happily assists his father in handing round drinks, while quite content with non-alcoholic drinks himself. However, even here there is a further stage to reach. He treats the adults as at his own level while treating contemporaries outside school as inferior. This father, who was once on the Surrey committee, gives a very perceptive account of his son's still somewhat immature social development.

A number of parents had had very serious problems in emotional development quite independent of any school. One was an old student of mine, so that I knew what a detailed study she had made of child development. Her first-born from weaning rejected the mother in favour of the father; when the father had to be away her experiences were terrible. Her own baby cowered away from her and rejected all food. 'You don't *know*,' she said, 'what it is like to be a normal, loving mother and to be totally rejected!' We discussed the situation at length when we met again a dozen years after our college association. Of course, she did not know then that this pining, cowering child was intellectually gifted. It seemed most probable that some inherited mechanism had gone wrong, such as with autistic children; it might have been associated with imprinting (when the mind registers things automatically). But as we talked he was now roaring down the garden in the trolley game. She had won through with the help of a child psychologist. It is, of course, a part of good psychological training to know when to call on experts. But in the first years she had herself won through sufficiently for him to attend school at five. She had, as we talked, two other gifted children romping round the garden, who had presented no such problem. It is only when parents have more than one child that they begin to relinquish their 'delusions of grandeur' about how much they make children what they are. But it is hard luck to have a child with such problems as the first-born. At the time of writing he is doing extremely well in one of our more famous public schools.

Another mother writes that her baby daughter, later proving to be very gifted, was 'difficult and demanding'. By seven and a half, she was depressed, unhappy and frustrated in the home. When this depressed girl was brought to me I said that, instead of talking to her as if seven-and-a-half, they should treat her as eleven-and-a-half. If they did not know how to do that they should watch adolescents and how they were successfully treated. This was advice which proved successful. I had also told them of unsuspected mathematical ability, and to do justice here they had had to persuade a well-known boys' prep school to allow her to join a small group of half a dozen girls there. 'She settled down happily,' writes the mother, 'and is doing very well.' She adds that the younger children, also both gifted, cause no bother. So here is another example of the first-born presenting unexpected problems, which do not emerge with younger members of the family.

There were several occasions when this advice to treat a child according to mental age had real meaning to parents and the emotional problems immediately evanesced. One was the girl who went through a bad patch at a good school, and was rescued by the headmaster with a senior school scholarship at the end of her two middle school years. The parents were treating her as eight and disobedient, so I suggested treating her as a student with suitable interests in her bedroom such as a student's desk close to plenty of bookshelves and display space for special interests (in this case very wide-ranging), a long mirror, and so on. Another girl was gangling and awkward and 'not like other children'. She had a professional father, clearly possessed of great inner resources. When the girl was out of earshot I told him she had an IQ too high to assess reliably, so we called it IQ 170+. At that moment the seven-year-old, as tall as most eleven-year-olds, came and laid her head on her seated father's shoulder. 'Was I all right?' she whispered. He just nodded and said, 'We do have some wonderful conversations, don't we?' I felt there was no need to worry there. In reply to my letter, I heard she had passed the Certificate of Education with honours, and been accepted at Millfield and Bedales but had chosen another distinguished school. She has passed grades five and six for piano, and had a star AAA award for all-round ability. She is attractive, and may become acting Head Girl – but her room is very untidy.

Another was a five-year-old boy whose very talented parents complained that he *argued* with them, and what was so terrible for them was that he was usually *right*. They said it was so bad for their morale. I was able to recommend treating him as eight, and this worked immediately. I suspect that this works for several reasons: when the parents know that the child is gifted they feel interested instead of threatened; when the child is appropriately treated he responds with ease instead of feeling frustrated; when both parents and child feel at ease, the relationship can move on to new and interesting developments; and lastly, it is no vague generalisation to say 'Look at children of your child's mental age', but a practical suggestion upon which they can act.

There are a few more examples of very difficult emotional situations. An able older sister, whose younger sister was brilliant, apparently felt severely threatened by the younger sister catching up on her so fast. The mother said they went through very stormy periods with the older girl, who only gave up the fixed idea that she was dull when I tested her and explained to her the level of her ability, which was IQ 146 ± 5. The mother says she works with 'extraordinary diligence' but has difficulty in her relationship with school contemporaries (also able), as well as her sister. The mother, a graduate, wished to teach art and had the greatest difficulty in getting the local college of education to accept the notion that 'a *graduate* would want to teach art' – a very unpleasant revelation of non-artistic man's contempt for art; or perhaps the non-graduate's unrealistic notions of graduation. However, this mother won, and confessed after some years of teaching that she would not know how to teach an isolated gifted child while attending to all the others. I suspect that what the mother diagnosed as the girl's great diligence is actually artistic perseveration, the tendency to continue in any activity once it is begun, until it is finished. This is a characteristic of all artists, and of scientists and mathematicians in creative phase. The girl under discussion plays several instruments and might well harness these intense feelings to the discipline of music.

Another mother describes a first-born, a boy so lacking in self-confidence that he is afraid to try anything new for fear of failing. With unusual penetration, the mother can see that this has had a severely constricting effect upon his interests. But the younger sister, gifted yet not as gifted as the boy, is not restricted, and has far more interests. Another mother describes a very difficult situation with an unusually bright first-born child : 'As a baby and a small child the most notable thing about him was his unpredictable reactions. Anything new or different frightened him, even when he was only a few months old, e.g. new faces, spectacles, someone wearing a hat, being taken to new places, or horror of horrors, being put in a different cot or pram ! From six months to two and a half years he suffered night terrors almost nightly. After two and a half years he began to settle down gradually, as we were able to communicate more easily.' At two the mother deduced that he had made friendly overtures to a cat in the garden and got scratched. She could tell 'from the tensions in his body as he approached the house that he was suppressing great distress'. This was the age at which he began to kick and hit his mother as the perpetrator of these irregularities. As soon as he could talk, he conveyed his highly sensitised awareness of danger; by three or four years he was advising his father not to park in a certain place and listing the specific obstruction dangers, or not to picnic in a certain field for fear of angering the farmer, and so on. There was nothing in the home to elicit this anxiety about angering others. Admittedly he was in part projecting his own unacceptable anger. A minor accident when a boy was knocked off a bicycle caused him greatest distress. From three to five he attended a very good playgroup but even beginning one day a week caused great strain. Yet children had always been in and out of the home. When a painting easel fell down, he ran away and hid from the very wise and understanding supervisor for a whole morning. Just before he had to go to the primary school he got the idea of rough-and-tumble games in playschool; and the parents knew they had succeeded. He was the one who came fourth in the selection test for Manchester Grammar School. But it was very wise of the parents not to impose a long journey on this exceptionally sensitive child, stable though he now appeared.

There is another account of emotional development which might help other parents. It concerns a boy, aged twelve, so good and successful and modest that one does not really notice that he is gifted. But he is indeed gifted. The mother writes that he:

> . . . is, I would think, a fairly standard prep school product – exceptional in that he is 'so thoroughly nice' (quote from head-master's report) . . . He fell deeply in love with a beautiful French girl I had staying last summer. She was seventeen, quite charming and greatly concerned at the effect she wrought. . . . He would sit by her for hours, listen to records, paint – and draw and endlessly discuss life's problems. He would become devoured by jealousy if other students occupied her attention, and nearly broke the jaw of a fifteen-year-old French boy whose manner he considered lacked proper deference. . . . The girl herself was remarkable in that she had a mesmeric effect on all, especially men. Apart from her beauty she possessed an extraordinary stillness, an other-worldliness that was positively hypnotic. . . .

A car-racing champion of France had been so obsessed by her that she had had to bring him to his senses by means of breaking a beer bottle over his head. As the time for this 'thoroughly nice' boy to return to school approached, his moods became so impossibly black that his very tolerant mother delivered a lecture. The outcome of that was that he and his Ophelia became officially engaged, the boy of twelve and the girl of seventeen, and everyone in the house party 'breathed normally'. They will not meet again for another year.

I have dealt with that at length because it bears a strange resemblance to what happened to Berlioz, only was less well handled by his mother. There was a house party in the mountains and Berlioz, aged about fourteen, fell deeply in love with a very beautiful married woman. It was a romantic period and everyone was very amused. Three years later, when Berlioz was seventeen, this lady let Frau Berlioz know that she was passing within a few miles and would take anything she wanted to the city. Frau Berlioz made up a parcel and sent her son to the carriage without saying whose carriage it was. He set off, striding over the mountains. But when he came back his face was so terrible that the mother greatly regretted her amusing little experiment. Berlioz never knew a happy marriage. He married Harriet Smithson after seeing her play Ophelia in a Paris season of Shakespeare, but opted out of the marriage seven years later. His attempt to master what was going on inside him can be heard in his Symphonie Fantastique, Op. 14.

The Ophelia myth, which appears in so many guises, is notably unrealistic in *Hamlet*. The Prince of Denmark is suffering the experience when he falls in love with the daughter of Polonius. First he idolises her and then, when she reveals human demands, he rejects her utterly as failing to conform to the myth. The English mother actually referred to the French girl as 'our Ophelia'. So many outstandingly able children learn to develop a hard exterior, that we tend to think of them as tough. This is very far from the truth, particularly when they are struggling with their own sensitivity. Adolescence is a time for able children which urgently needs high-level research. The romantic age in which Berlioz lived was, by modern standards, unrealistic. We are much more anxious today to find out what children are really like, in order to see how to treat them.

One father made some points that are well worth reading:

1 (a) To what degree are we able to ascertain that the child needs something 'extra' or 'alternative' to the normal local school provided by the education authorities?

   (b) If it is merely an 'extra', can this be provided by the home rather than attempting to send the child to a more suitable school – a transplant to a semi-alien situation?

2   If a different school is needed — determined by objective testing and professional advice – then the child should be prepared for repeated testing . . . heads of schools, county organisers, educational psychologists, should all be made aware of the child and his/her problem.

3   When the child has been independently tested and this has confirmed one's own opinion of ability, then *false* humility is quite out of place. Join the local NAGC groups – talk to parents of similar children – the parents are often the experts. Send the child to camps, on trips, to day courses, etc., arranged by the NAGC.

4   If you know of clever or brilliant people, they will very often be quietly delighted to discuss the child. They often know all too well the problems of being 'alone', of antagonising adults or older children with one's superior knowledge or ability. They are not likely to be over-awed or 'threatened' by the child's brilliance — a sad state of affairs in schools, too often.

5   My wife's advice is – 'build your lives around the children'. Personally we have tried to do this.

That advice comes from a very quiet-spoken schoolmaster. It will touch the hearts of those who have had to conceal the facts of ability from neighbours, as if being gifted were something to sweep under the carpet.

Many whose children are in the care of understanding teachers, mostly at advanced public schools, express immense gratitude for the good fortune of having the children so well placed. But others really lament school boredom. One mother says that we should accept the comments made by the gifted children themselves. Her daughter told her that the most boring part of the school was the lessons; and the best part was working on your own. The boy who taught himself to play a violin at five is, at the time of writing, eight and has played many times in public by now: the Allegro by Fiocco; the Sonata in E major by Handel; the complete three movements of the second Violin Concerto in E major by Bach; and he has been deputy-leader of a county school orchestra, and in their concerts played two movements of the Golden Sonata by Purcell. His father is now in charge of the NAGC children in a public school. The boy was accepted by the King's College, Cambridge, choir school, but they withdrew this as it meant a change of violin teacher, and he is going to St Paul's Choir School. But he has to wait a while. How does he pass the time out of school when not playing? He has long since taught himself the squares (up to 20) and now is experimenting with change of base from binary to duodecimal. 'This,' says his father, 'all learned out of sheer boredom through lack of daily challenge.'

A mother who is a teacher says her daughter was talking fluently at two-and-a-quarter, counting well, and more like a child of four or five. The mother was able to recognise this as not average behaviour. The girl was adopted and two years later went with the parents to the adoption society to 'collect' a six-weeks-old brother. All the same, after two days she suggested returning him. 'We have had him long enough!' She has always been jealous of him, but at the same time fiercely protective and motherly towards him.

The child who was accustomed to a slide rule at four made requests in keeping with her ability, when six, for Christmas: a magnetic compass in order to find distance and bearing of pirate treasure; and an experimental kit. They chose an electricity set, as less dangerous than chemistry. She is very interested in physics and astronomy.

These accounts of how parents are helping their outstanding children at home show great insight. The high-level intellectual stimulus they are giving seems more like tutorials of a later stage of good schooling. As schools are at present run, the busy teachers

have a full-time job in arranging the education of the main body
of the large classes, of average, or near average, ability. A way
must be found in the last quarter of the twentieth century to
nourish the gifted children and the artistically talented ones.

A matter of which we are in urgent need of information is the
learning curve of exceptionally able children. It appears to sweep
up in an exponential curve, leaving an infuriated teacher far below
like the hen in the children's story, whose ducklings horrify her by
taking to water, to her 'the wrong element'. One mother of
mathematically gifted children said we need to know more of the
passing enthusiasms of gifted adolescents. Another described a succession of enthusiasms, '. . . for instance horse-riding ! she was very
keen, mastered the art, reached quite a high standard, and then
lost interest The next was flute-playing – again enthusiasm up to
being able to play sufficiently well for her own amusement, and
then, no more. Swimming was also a great favourite, for a limited
time.' The mother speculates whether this is a characteristic of
gifted children. In a way, it is typical of all adolescents. But what
seems to puzzle parents and teachers is the apparent waste of
making such strides and then casting aside what could be a valuable asset.

The answer may lie in the fact that the learner and the teacher
are in the learning situation for different reasons. The teacher expects the child – particularly such a quick-learning child – to become a good flautist. But the motive for the boundlessly curious
gifted child may be something quite different: he or she may just
want to know how you get the various sounds from the flute – and
how you get them from the oboe or the double bass. So naturally
child and teacher lose rapport. One thing is certain: in our present
state of ignorance, the teacher has to be a very, very quick
learner. As we saw in Chapter 4 with music, the teacher has to
distinguish between the performer for whom a particular accomplishment is to develop into a way of life, and the one for whom
this accomplishment is to be an enjoyable hobby. Teacher and
parents all have to clarify their thinking about what one might
call 'delusions of star-launching'. This is why the father of the
five-year-old who taught himself to play the violin said objective
assessment is necessary. We have already seen that a group of two

or three experts, working as a team, can give objective assessment of art in a different way from objective assessment of intelligence.

One father said we should give more attention to the problems of parents who were not themselves gifted. My own experience here has been that almost every parent of gifted and/or talented children with whom I have had the privilege of working thinks that is their own situation. They are on the whole extraordinarily modest but also very shrewd. One wise and intelligent mother, an editor and very sensitive to music, commented sadly upon her gifted daughter, that she could see her passing through all her piano grades without difficulty; but she would remain unmusical at the end. For her it was just a mildly interesting intellectual exercise. This is contrary to public opinion. One has to go into very deep analysis of the situation to see how envy of parents with gifted children prejudices thinking by others. One reason for writing this book is to show some of the problems of having such children, thus arousing sympathy for the families, rather than envy. An example from a mother with two outstanding daughters will show the deep modesty that many feel. 'I know,' she writes, 'that they will outstrip me. But meanwhile they have each other, and they still have to be children, at the moment.' This takes us into the realms of wisdom and insight, of comprehension of experience, by no means the prerogative of the intellectually brilliant. Another mother, again with two brilliant daughters, just puts her finger on the need to be children. 'You have,' she writes, 'to look as if you have all the time in the world to listen, and to have inexhaustible reserves of odd materials to aid sudden inspirations for activities.' But this last mother also wrote how lovely and mind-stretching it was to have the splendid discussions, even though the child rushed off to make dolls' clothes for a beloved little cousin, or to design a harness for the pony to pull a sleigh converted to a troika (which worked on the one weekend morning of snow). Being an attentive listener, a sounding board for their thinking, is something we have to give all children. Children learn attention by being given attention. This is a different process from answering questions.

Maybe some of the comments made by this group of parents will help others in the same predicament. As one mother put it: it would have helped to know that these children often need less sleep and suffer frustration at school, and she now saw that other mothers were wrong in accusing *her* of being neurotic. One pair made a most determined effort to stop their daughter reading far into the night. The child had always been an avid reader – she is the one who was a fluent speaker at two-and-a-quarter – and persistently read quite late. They felt she was getting too little sleep and persuaded her not to read late. But then she could not sleep at all, so they hastily lifted the ban. Had they but known of the two boys with their differing periods of wakefulness, they could have been grateful that such a quiet occupation as reading was preferred.

Incidentally, there is a tip about reading in bed which concerns all children and cannot be given too often. Every few months, alter the bed and/or the light, so that the spine has a chance to curve the other way. This is particularly valuable for children who spend perhaps twenty hours a week reading in bed.

There is a point which may ring a bell with many who did not think of mentioning it. The matter of tidiness arose in connection with two boys living almost at opposite ends of England. A father, himself a meticulous, orderly man, writes, 'Untidy. Not only in dress; writing and letter-forming disgraceful (due to speed of committing thoughts to paper) – no loss of accuracy but distasteful at first glance. Cannot see that presentation and first impressions matter – will argue that content and depth of examination of subject is of paramount importance.' A mother, also a trim person, writes, 'Now at twelve, in contrast to his early timidity he appears to be bold, and fearless and quite an extrovert. He is usually dirty and untidy. He has no interest whatever in appearances. In fact he scorns any pride in appearance and entreaties to care for possessions. Sadly his school work reflects this attitude and is careless and unpleasing.' The father, himself a punctilious man, also found this untidiness distasteful.

Two personal incidents come to my mind. The first is when we were children and walking to church. I heard my mother say to my father, 'Just look at that new cap! It looks as if he has deliberately jumped on it in a puddle!' That is exactly what my brother, who attended an Elizabethan Grammar School, had told me he had done. With, to me, disconcerting insight she sighed and said, 'I suppose I should not have embarrassed him with a new cap.' The other incident concerned the son of a colleague, long before all the young chose to look moth-eaten. She had bought him jeans, at his request, to attend a local distinguished art college. Suddenly nobody could have a bath because the jeans were bleaching. She was mystified and a little anxious that he might make a fool of himself. Shortly afterwards, she took some students to the British Museum, and there they saw a group of students drawing Egyptian exhibits. When she returned she described this and said, 'My dear! It is a rigid uniform. Rigid as the dress of hussars.'

Returning to the two untidy boys, who should be attaining success worthy of their gifts, the first boy really has the ace card when he advises his father not to be so superficial, but to go for essentials; and the second boy does not show indifference to tidiness, but active resistance. I myself, as a teacher who for twenty years showed children how to enjoy the mechanics and rhythm of writing, am naturally in favour of tidiness. But these boys are showing signs of serious revolt. I would set out to get some inside information to see if this untidy writing, too, turns out to be a matter of rigid conformity. This is one of those delicate situations when what is required is understanding. Action can wait. Then when action seems propitious I would choose a moment of exceptionally good rapport to 'leak' the information that I now know why the child must be untidy. In other words, I suspect that untidiness is one of those phenomena where some gifted children can get their urgently needed social living by doing exactly the same as other children. The next stage, to put the matter on a discussion level, could wait for a year or two, as the gifted children are so often below subsistence level in approval from classmates.

This way of handling what looks, to parents and teachers alike, irrational behaviour, can often bypass the first rather clumsy attempts to preserve individuality against elders. Because lack of tidiness is specifically mentioned, it is described in detail. But the adolescent barriers come up over many other aspects, such as near-insolence, or casualness over other people's property. The children would not dare begin to show their vacillating independence at all, but for the support of their friends, who are also making their first break-away from home. Whatever the fashion, long hair or short hair, pinstriped trousers or tatty jeans, if this is seen as growth towards society away from home, it helps. Parents, no longer feeling threatened, can enjoy the natural developments instead of exacerbating them. Only by letting them loose from their parents and teachers can we help them through the stages of social conformity, and on their way to true independence of living. First they have to conform with their home, accepting what their parents think of them. Then they have to conform with their friends. Lastly they should allow themselves to be what they really are.

An unexpected bonus in the replies by parents was to discover how vividly the children recalled their visits to my home. This is in part due to the phenomenal memories of gifted children; but the parents gratuitously mentioned how much the children appreciated being treated at their true level as persons. This is a special characteristic of the NAGC activities, whenever and wherever they are carried out. The brothers with different sleeping patterns came when they were three and eight. Their mother wrote that they often refer to the house with all the electronic gadgets and seem to remember all they saw quite clearly. A father wrote that his two children have not forgotten a single detail.

They probably recognised in my husband a kindred spirit. He was educated at a public school that was founded in the mid-sixteenth century. By fifteen years of age, he became an item on the governors' agenda for expulsion. The list of his offences seemed endless, and included reaching the school cantilever clock to put time and strike independently wrong. But what caused most trouble was his creeping into chapel one Saturday night to link every stop of the organ to the *vox humana* stop. Nobody knew till the service began and the whole chapel shook. Most of the governors were more than prepared to dismiss this troublesome boy. But one, an old boy of the school, was John Reith, later to be head of the British Broadcasting Corporation. He asked to see the boy and their conversation was exclusively about how he had managed, a few weeks before, to send a concert over the air to a

friend who was ill in bed about forty miles away. After he had
become head of the BBC, Reith used this method of outside broadcasting; and outside broadcasts are today basically on the same
principle as this boy invented. There is an important lesson for
adults here. If we pick these brilliant children's brains, let us do
better than Reith and acknowledge our sources. We have to set
these children true standards of professional conduct.

Without doubt, the children recognised themselves in him. They
would run after him calling, 'Christopher! Christopher!' as if they
had always known him. When their parents said anxiously that
this was not the way to behave, they would say with puzzled
expressions, 'But he is my friend!' They invented things to show
him, and he sat back and roared with laughter at each one. There
was one that particularly delighted him, as it was a device for
extracting money from grandfathers. At the age of ten he had
himself been rescued from a preparatory school and educated by
a brilliant grandfather who said he should be coached for common
entrance. This invention needed a penny to operate its elaborate
mechanism, and once the penny had slipped down, only the
inventor could retrieve it. One Surrey boy was driven down the
lane and told that an autistic computed from Stuttgart was in the
laboratory undergoing speech therapy. The boy was so inspired
that he wrote the following poem for his birthday:

Poem for Mr Bailey

Computer Computer please type me
   a rhyme
If I mend you and tune you
   Will you do it in time?
Do it slowly and carefully make
   Sure you don't explode
I don't want to be lying on my back
   in the road
It's printing a message and guess
   who its to?
It says 'Happy birthday' and of course
   its to you.

I was unable to trace the poet so have not got permission to include it. I have left punctuation untouched and omitted the name, but should add that I found the poem in my husband's papers, which was a clear token of his appreciation. Both these last two boys, the extractor of pennies from grandfather and the computer poet, were assessed by someone else, so I was unable to include them on my graph, when they would have had very high positions.

While all this was going on in my area, similar work was being done in other areas of the country. It is very remarkable that the NAGC survived those first years. Many times it looked like exploding with frustration. Society did not expect to have any gifted children who were unable to find their way to the university through the correct scholarship system. I was called in because, after some stormy sessions in committee at the London Institute of Education Teachers' Centre, I had persuaded them to run a course of talks on gifted children. I had come across Terman's work at Stanford University, California, in the early thirties, when co-principal of a school with average IQ 128. I knew that the facts would have to come out here, too, about non-conforming children of highest ability, and the teachers would have to be prepared for them. It was a worry to me that still, after thirty years, even the Froebel Institute, which had nurtured me as a progressive teacher, seemed unsympathetic. But I badgered the principal on behalf of the children and they accepted us two or three Saturday mornings in a term. These visits went on for years, and here again the children particularly appreciated being treated at their true level.

If I had to pinpoint the meaning of these visits to the Froebel Institute for the children, it was the unique social experience at two levels: courteous discussion with students (a feature of the old Froebel movement was to treat children as persons), and the fun of playing with children who could see what you were talking about while themselves saying things worth hearing. One boy with IQ 170+ was furious at the suggestion of a school on a *Saturday*. But he agreed to come once only, to see if it really was like 'horrid old school'. As we talked our way round the lovely grounds this seven-year-old danced up to his mother, came within an inch, whispered with shining eyes, 'I'm coming next Saturday,' and was gone. Children who had missed their footing in relations with other children got the idea here that it was fun to play with other children; and school situations improved because the gifted ones ceased to withdraw – at least in play. One mother was highly amused that they travelled all this way for her son to play football for two hours with another gifted boy. But he is now in a public school of brilliant academic record. For a couple of terms, never having learned to work at school, he came bottom; then he got the idea of working and came top.

As stated earlier, this chapter was circulated in manuscript to all parents who had responded. When this mother of the small footballer returned the papers she made some very interesting comments on her son, whom I had only known in the hurly-burly of the NAGC activities. Like the boy (p. 115) who was so scared when tiny, by the time her son was three months old, he would cry with obvious terror until he was sick when in a strange place, in a friend's garden or on the local common. Even her husband would not believe it till he took the child out in the pram alone. When they told the doctor, he just laughed scoffingly. This lasted till he was two, and she had begun to think he might be autistic. 'Thankfully,' she writes, 'he was not our first child, or I should have thought I was not a mother.' She knows of two cases where such a situation arose with a first child, and other children came before the mothers had established good relations. By the time these two first-born children were ten and twelve, the parents clearly resented the children, who had made them failures as parents. But of her own son, now also succeeding in a public school, she says he still suffers acute apprehension, but will screw up his courage, in order to carry out what he has decided he must do. The older sister is serene and avid for fresh adventures.

A matter which was often discussed with parents was whether the children should know that they were gifted, and if so when and how they should be told. My own lines of thinking are these:

1 Young children are not really involved in what other children are doing or thinking of them until about seven, when the 'gang stages' begins. Therefore gifted children can be given advanced individual work without others noticing or feeling resentful.

2 The old puritanical idea that if you are gifted you have to pay something back to society does not belong to modern ideas of child development. All children enjoy responsibility, provided the responsibility is neither too much nor too little. For children, as it should be for adults, responsibility should be equated with privilege.

3 The first to notice that others are being 'stupid' will be the gifted children. We all know gifted adults who regard themselves as normal and everyone else as quite extraordinarily stupid. They have not been given help about their own giftedness at the right moment.

There is no set chronological age for revealing to the child these special gifts. When the moment seems right, parents should take care to be in good rapport and to sound very casual. The accent should be taken off the child himself to the fact that there are great individual differences in heredity and environment. Equal opportunity does not mean identical opportunity, but a chance to develop in the way best suited to an individual. Some people try very hard and do not achieve great success, others may try less hard and succeed.

The able child needs to know his parents' philosophy of life, and help them to develop it further. He is already at the stage where he has outgrown babyish rules, and he may want to make his own rules, for instance in Monopoly, so that it is impossible for too much property to get into the hands of one person. He is beginning to see that what he took for justice and injustice as a baby can be observed in another light now. There is a sentence in Bronowski's (1958) *Science and Human Values* which might help. 'The values by which we are to survive,' he writes, 'are not rules for just and unjust conduct, but are those deeper illuminations in whose light justice and injustice, good and evil, means and ends are seen in fearful sharpness of outline.'

At the time when I sent out requests to parents whose replies constitute the main body of this chapter, I expected to hear that many of the children were very bored in school, unless they were fortunate enough to attend progressive schools. One thing is certain; the teachers cannot be blamed for this sad situation. Special training is necessary for the task of educating gifted children. I knew that in 1973 the college of the London Institute of Education were submitting to the Institute suggestions for a new curriculum, now that trained teachers were to be granted degrees. Two of my former colleagues helped me make a list of all the people to whom I might make a personal approach, in an inquiry as to whether the term 'gifted children' was appearing anywhere in their suggestions, if only as a suggested area of special education which might be studied in depth. This moment of transition is very difficult for them all.

I wrote to the thirty-four colleges of education which belong to the London Institute of Education, using where possible a personal approach, and asked each if they could spare time to scribble a note on the back of my letter, as to whether gifted children were being mentioned in any way whatsoever in the curriculum suggestions. Eighteen of the thirty-four colleges replied. Four said gifted children were not mentioned in the syllabus. Fourteen colleges said that the term did appear or that the subject was bound to come up in the psychology course. It is quite clear that the majority of teachers in training are not yet getting the help they need on the special requirements of gifted children. However, one of the best investigations so far has come from one of the London colleges. It is fully described in Bridges (1969), *Gifted Children and the Brentwood Experiment*. Moreover, the Froebel Institute gave most valuable help in the early days. A number of colleges are now giving help in different parts of the country, and their students will not be disconcerted at finding one or two gifted children in a class.

There is a wealth of information in the correspondence with the parents which could not be included, as it would have expanded this chapter too much. If anyone is interested to follow up the suggested research in the second paragraph of this chapter on the parents and their children, permission to see the correspondence could be sought. But it would have to be high-level research for such permission to be granted. One mother asked to be spared replying as her very brilliant son, now at a technical college, was having a welcome spell of treatment as a normal person. One father, himself holding a responsible post in a London college, suggested that colleges of further education would be a good place to search for school-failures now being redeemed. The Open University would certainly be another useful area for such findings. But the first priority is to find as many as we can of the gifted and talented, while they are still very young.

6

WHAT OF THE FUTURE?

Those who care for gifted children very rightly feel that they are pioneers in a new field. This is strange, since we have established that it was specifically the gifted boys alone who were educated in these islands, from the time the Romans were here. It is not the concept of an able child that is new, but the plight into which many of them have fallen since the introduction of universal education in 1872. The speed with which the brightest children get through their work is intolerable to most busy teachers, who are doing their best to teach the rest of the class the same material, which most of them find very taxing. So the gifted child is told to get on, to do it again, to do up his shoes or wash his hands, in fact, do anything but interrupt again. Thus when the poet Robert Graves was a little boy his father found him in tears because it was so boring learning the twenty-three times table. This manner of quieting a gifted child was known before the invention of the alphabet. The brightest boys of Ur of the Chaldees had to learn their forty-nine times table in about 2000 BC. Maybe this was a contributory cause of Abraham's emigration from Ur. He certainly had a number of characteristics now being studied in connection with gifted children: he was a natural leader, ingenious in problem-solving; his conception had been late in his father's life; and – a matter now receiving an increasing amount of informed attention – he could interpret symbols, because, in an age when fathers or leaders of groups actually killed the sons who seemed to be a threat to their authority, he saw that the ritual slaying of a ram could represent the actual slaying of a first-born. He also made the mighty abstraction of monotheism.

There is a qualitative as well as a quantitative difference of the learning of able children. They learn much more than children of less ability and can recall what they have learned much more easily; but their ability to think in abstractions gives them, not just a short cut, but seven-league boots to move at speeds far beyond the speed of others. Their surveying capacity is as unexpected as a knight's move to a row of pawns; and it is done on high-level abstraction networks of thinking. Those who attended the first conference of NAGC will recall the account by the headmaster of Millfield of his interview with a seven-year-old who wanted to come to the school to study algebra. Why? Because he had been told it was a series of short cuts. When the headmaster was called away, he handed the boy an algebra book. Half an hour later he returned to find the boy standing at the window, the book closed upon the table. So much for a desire to study algebra, thought the headmaster. He asked how the boy had enjoyed the book. 'Wonderful! Marvellous!' cried the boy with shining eyes. 'It is not only a system of short cuts. It is a further system of short cuts with short cuts! But,' he continued courteously, 'I don't know whether you would agree with me. I found the third chapter the weakest.' The conference was informed that the third chapter was generally considered to be the weakest.

The United States Congressional Record for 30 January 1974 reports a girl who had looked forward to school but by about twelve was so withdrawn that she failed seventh grade maths. The school said she was mentally retarded, and it took no interest in her delight with compound trigonometry fractions. The parents talked to the President of the Association for the Mentally Retarded in their State and were told that such able children are *frequently* referred to them. It seems that, like the legendary absent-minded professor, these children may withdraw from all incoming sense impressions, such as hearing and seeing, to engage in some complex abstraction, and have a singularly vacant expression while this is happening. Hence the teacher's wrong diagnosis. But there is something else to alarm the teacher. What if he or she has never done compound trigonometry fractions? The whole authority of the teacher is, rightly or wrongly, built upon his inexhaustible knowledge, unless he is a truly progressive teacher. In that case he can easily say, 'Ah, I have not found out about this yet. Let us find an authority to help you.'

The fact that an individual gifted child can *frequently* be so misjudged, raises the question of selecting those who are gifted. Before the invention of the alphabet, it seems, rote memory was used in learning extra tables; and after the invention of the alphabet, a rote alphabetic reading capacity was used, perhaps simultaneously with the tables. By and large this would be not too bad a selection technique, though we now know that this would have been more successful with girls than boys. But it was rather like finding gold and never mining it, finding the most intelligent boys and then doing nothing further to educate them. We would do well at this point to remember that our present selection techniques leave much to be desired. There has been a great improvement in assessment of intelligence during the twentieth century, largely due to the researches of Burt in the UK and Terman in the US. But, as we have seen, the important artistic side has proved much more intractable. So, many people have falsely restored their self-respect by denegrating the importance of art. Artistic sensitivity is essential for leadership. It is no good being surrounded by intellectuals who draw up fantastic designs for Utopia, and then to have no leader to say, 'Nonsense! Humans won't do things that way. They want to be in Utopia alongside the intellectuals, but they have to approach with feeling. Let me handle them.' When Churchill said that all he offered was 'blood, sweat and tears', professional political actor that he was, he had first rehearsed each cadence and pause of that speech with his remarkable wife. But his public school pushed him out. It appears that great men have attained prominence *in spite of their education*.

George Steiner (1970) told us in *Bluebeard's Other Castle* that the sado-sexual fantasies of the nineteenth century would inevitably, as the fantasies wore thin with over-use, turn into the reality tortures of the twentieth century. Poets like D. H. Lawrence wrote of it before the worst had come. But there is another side to this thinking and dreaming which progresses to reality. Creative thinking can also lead on, but to more constructive reality. So we make up our minds, in what we know to be a state of ignorance, as to what we mean by a gifted and talented child, and then set to work on high-level research to find out what develops the individual

of potential gifts and talents. This will raise the probability that
the potential of our able children will be developed. Moreover, it
may be developed faster than now seems possible. As one goes
carefully through the papers on gifted and talented children published in the United States, these papers published in 1970 saying
there was no federal support, no money, no personnel and so on,
were obsolete a couple of years later. They had money, and government support, and personnel in ten of the fifty states. It is very
much easier to get to where you want to go, if you find out just
where your objective is. Since we are, here, not yet as advanced
governmentally as the Americans, let us examine their definition
of gifted and talented children:

Gifted and talented children are those identified by pro-
fessionally qualified persons who, by virtue of outstanding
abilities, are capable of high performance. These are children
who require differentiated educational programs and/or ser-
vices beyond those normally provided by the regular school
program in order to realize their contribution to self and
society.

Children capable of high performance include those with
demonstrated achievement and/or potential ability in any of
the following areas, singly or in combination: general intellectual ability; specific academic aptitude; creative or productive thinking; leadership ability; visual and performing
arts, and psychomotor ability.

It can be assumed that the utilization of these criteria for
identification of the gifted and talented will encompass a
minimum of three to five per cent of the school population.
Report to Congress by US Commissioner of Education,
November 1971

The Americans put in many decades of work before they could
persuade Congress to take an interest in especially able children.
But they were greatly helped by the Russians sending up their first
Sputnik in 1957. They more or less told the Government that the
Russians took care of their supernormal children, so what could
you expect? By 1973 they were laughing officially at this. The

Assistant Secretary for Education, giving a nationwide talk on the education of the gifted, called his address, *Send Up More Sputniks*, and recounted how a few days ago he had explained to a group of visiting Russian educationists what a help their Sputnik had been, in the American campaign for able children. What the Sputnik was as a spur to government in the US, the US Congressional achievements for the gifted can be to the British and their government. We have to plan a long-term strategy, but success in America should shorten the time we need to wait for substantial governmental help. With the introduction of the scholarship system for brighter children in 1893, and establishment of the necessity to teach individual children according to ability and aptitude in the Education Act of 1944, we had what able children require on our statute books very early indeed. Now what we have to plan is the implementation of these ideas, which includes tapping Government financial sources.

All pioneers know the obstruction they meet from people who are unwilling to help but not everyone realises that this obstruction is largely due to man's inertia and egotism, rather than a firm conviction promoting a skilled strategy. Life seems very difficult for most people, and they feel they can just manage if they are allowed to go on as they have taught themselves to do. There is a great waste of energy in mistaking this for anything but inertia. Lorenz, in *King Solomon's Ring*, gives a wonderful example of the great difficulty in having to break down old habits and make new ones, with path-habit formation in shrews, which crystallises the problem for us. In a chapter called 'The Taming of the Shrew', he reports the behaviour of some shrews who find a slight change in their customary route. In any strange surroundings, they go step by step, whiskering nervously right and left, until after a few repeats of utmost exactitude, they can proceed at great speed. By then the path-habit is as strictly bound as a railway engine to its track. There was one track with two stones which the shrews were accustomed to jumping on and off. So Lorenz waited until they had learned the path, and then moved the stones away. Each shrew jumped right up into the air in the place where the stones had been, and came down with a jarring bump. Each one returned carefully to whisker about, then went back to try again. It was only after the second fall through stoneless air that they began to suspect that the first fall had not been due to an error on their part, but to changed circumstances. Our need to remember what we have learned makes us very reluctant to unlearn and forget what we have once successfully learned.

We cannot disguise the fact that we are definitely challenging the established educational system of which we have rightly been proud for over a century. This is a threat to the establishment equivalent to removing a stone and demanding the troublesome business of forming new path-habits. The challenge is not over the concept of education for all, but over a small minority which is not yet receiving its statutory right to education according to ability and aptitude. The biographer of the art historian, now Lord Clark, says bluntly, 'For Kenneth Clark, as for other talented men, his school days were an unimportant period.' Divergent thinkers of today are looking for ways to remedy this disastrous situation; and in so doing, they must differentiate between inertia and reasoned opposition. Time and again communities through the ages have collapsed through starvation of original thought and overindulgence of inertia. We do not know much about the children of the past but we do know that, where great men have broken through, they usually had supportive families. Blake and Wordsworth each had a sister to believe in him; Van Gogh had a brother to market his pictures; Edison had a mother to take him from his school, when the teacher said he was not 'able' for education. The list of examples is very long indeed. Society has relished the idea that those unduly talented should be made to suffer and even become insane, in order to prove how wrong it is not to conform.

In the light of all this, we have to take a new look at our gifted drop-outs. Some very distinguished men have been drop-outs for a while. Robert Graves, who when seven had been bored at having to learn his twenty-three times table, became a drop-out; and some would say he never came back. Jacob Bronowski, when a refugee in the East End of London, was made to sit in the infant class till he could speak Engliish; and he wept. Later he joined Robert Graves as a drop-out for a couple of years. Our personalities have evolved through millions and millions of years, dependent on fierce anger as the dynamo for self-preservation. If this anger is not sufficiently channelled into self-discipline, to ensure freedom from and acceptance by the community within which we find ourselves, there are only two possibilities: either the anger turns in so that the individual withdraws to a world of unrealistic fantasies, or it turns out with equally unrealistic destructive behaviour. For a century we have thought these unco-operative youngsters in the wrong. Maybe they are so; but without doubt the elders are more in the wrong for projecting all blame upon the drop-outs and delinquents. Adult duty is to try to understand the causes; and to decide whether there are genuine injustices, in which case it is society which should be changed. Creativity dies in a society which can no longer adapt to fresh constructive demands.

Interest in able children is growing, largely through the pioneering of the NAGC. The attention and sympathy of the public is being roused, because it is the public which must vote for a manifesto including suitable education for these children. What we need are regional teams headed by experts all over the country. The eight regions of the Redcliffe–Maud report suggest themselves as a start, since the population research for this already enables us to work out expectancy of children of high ability in these regions. The NAGC already has the support of wealthy and distinguished organisations and individuals, forming an impressive list of supporters. The regional teams would require offices and consultants, and power to disseminate information and execute plans. This would rescue the children from their present plight of being locked in by a dead weight of structural and administrative restrictions. Moreover, society would be helped to overcome its hostility to disruptions of inertia.

As we have seen, experts already know how to make quite reliable selection of the children on the intellectual side; and these same experts know the most modern techniques so far for selecting the children of ablest artistic talent. But we are in urgent need of high-level postgraduate research on both what these children are like and what kind of education would best bring out their potential. Another area which claims our attention is the able children to be found amongst the many minorities of handicap:

the poor, the immigrant, the physically and perceptually handicapped, such as the spastic and blind and deaf. Experts in these minorities have to come forward and insist on the rights for the ablest in these groups as well. There is in America an Office of Education with a Director for the Education of the Gifted and Talented at Washington DC 20202. Ten of their states had an official representative within a year of the Congress financial assistance, and many others were almost ready for an official representative. Thus, from the Washington office a wealth of material is already available. There is a bibliography of US books on gifted and talented children, and another on handicapped children, with titles of books covering gifted and/or talented blind children, and so on. There are guides to such resources as are available, which are impressive by our standards. There is a list of advisory people and phone numbers for every state, whether there is an official representative or not. There are many leaflets and pamphlets from which speakers on the gifted and talented can obtain the latest information. The Americans also have a system of Exploration Scholarships, jointly with private non-profit groups. Thus one can see that the pioneering continues after the state begins to take over, which ensures no backsliding into inertia before firm running conditions for able children are established.

Working towards such organisation is the kind of strategy now needed for British children. When we come to examine, for instance, actual details of the impressive American programmes, of course we shall find differences in teaching techniques. But thinking in terms of the children themselves, we know that they would rather follow even a programmed piece of learning unaided, than sit in the terrible boredom to which so many are now condemned here. At one of the NAGC's centres south of London, a member of the committee said to the chairman that his son had been commanded in his junior school not to ask any more questions on mathematics. The chairman pointed out that he would be at his new London secondary school, of considerable fame, within months. There he could ask all the questions he liked, because the mathematics specialist would explain many of the answers. Before the first half-term the boy returned from the new school to say that he had been instructed to stop asking his *clever-clever* questions. The chairman got very angry and said that the father should get the undergraduate programme of the *Encyclopaedia Britannica* for mathematics. He found that he could hire it and within two years, that is to say when the boy was thirteen years old, just when he was reaching the stage of finals for a BSc degree in mathematics, the school found out. Some chord of shame must have been touched, because the school made him a prefect. This did not help his mathematics; but it satisfied a great need by making him socially acceptable with boys and masters.

There is a further point about this boy's need for social acceptance. The father said he was puzzled when the boy was asked some question in mathematics that his class was going to do the next day. Father and son were in the 'one in many thousands' class of intelligence, each with special mathematical ability. The father found his son's mind utterly entrancing, and delighted in explaining to someone who was so quick to understand. But there always came a time when the son held up his hand and said, 'Thank you! Stop! That is all I want now.' The father said indignantly to the chairman, 'There is *me* to consider! *I* know more! Why do I have to stop before the end?!' The committee discussed this and thought perhaps the boy loved to learn with his classmates, but the pace was so intolerably slow that he could not endure it. By this method he could join in the current stage, more than half thinking of other things, and end by being as ignorant as all the other boys about what came next. The father was able to check later, and found this to be the correct explanation of the behaviour.

Now let us take another close-up look at a small area of American work, this time how one education officer applies the help he gets from public and private sectors, concerning gifted and talented children. The author was in California in 1973 and able to ask many questions, within months of official help being announced by Congress. Cupertiono is just south of San Francisco and the education officer was Bruce de Vries. He had 25,000 children in the forty schools of Cupertiono. In the American definition of able children (see p. 144), it is stated that a *minimum* of 2 to 3 per cent of children are expected to be gifted or talented. Actually, those concerned with the children are looking for 10 to 12 per cent who might need special education suited to their ability and aptitudes. A tenth of the children in Cupertiono would be 2,500. The education officer said proudly that they had found 2,000, and were very pleased, although they knew there must be many more. This was the opposite of the attitude of the British educational authorities until the NAGC began to publicise the real plight of these children. The British were shutting their eyes and saying they were just the same as other children and no special measures were necessary. In Cupertiono some hundreds of the ones discovered so far were in regular classes, receiving extra help from the teacher. There were forty-seven special classes for children with IQ over 140. There were special centres where children went for half a day a week, and a steady 700 children were going through these centres each week. The children had a wide variety of exploration possibilities in the centres to choose from, and the teachers were picked with extra care. Every week the teachers concerned with the children of ability met together to discuss problems among themselves, share ideas, and stimulate each other. At these meetings they met many kinds of specialists.

With this help, able children at Cupertiono were being encouraged to become leaders, athletes and scholars. The British have been as suspicious about the training of high leadership talent as about the training of high intelligence. The fixed concept which has to be broken down is that people of leadership quality have to prove themselves by bursting the bonds of conformity themselves. This only results in personal ambition. What has to replace this outdated notion is a far subtler and productive technique for selecting leaders, resulting in better leadership. For instance, a point of discussion might well be that none should command who do not first know the humility of obeying. If we are able to have talented and trained leaders by the end of the twentieth century, we just might be able to re-direct the wrong turn international affairs have taken. But that could be too late. Cupertiono is just one of the towns which benefits from the $200,000 the US Congress has set aside for adapting part of the schools syllabus to the requirements of gifted children. Educational authorities are expected to spend 30 per cent of their allocation on hardware, materials, and field trips.

In 1973 the California Association for the Gifted, the American counterpart of one of our branches of the NAGC, held its Eleventh Annual Conference, lasting two days. Speakers, governmental as well as educational, came from all over the United States and the theme was Individualizing for the Gifted. A run-through some of the titles of talks and workshops gives an indication of the care with which they are training their teachers for this work:

The Gifted and Talented
Exploration Center for the Gifted – some ideas
Self-directed Learning Tasks
Adapting the Curriculum for the Gifted
Filming for the Gifted
I was a Teenage Film-maker
Talent Tutors Talent
Name of the Game is Reading
Any Librarian Can !
Make Math Meaningful
Identifying Highly Gifted Math Students.

The Americans are not just leaving it to the teacher to ignore or struggle with the gifted and talented. All of the ten states with a full-time expert in charge of the education of the gifted had something similar going on. Other states might not be quite so advanced as California, the state in which Terman of Stanford University and his team evolved, to a high level, individual assessment of intelligence and, amongst other matters, made follow-up studies of their gifted children.

In 1971, according to a Congress Report, 75 per cent of the able children who were receiving special care were in the ten states which a couple of years later were to have governmental support with a full-time expert in charge of outstandingly able children. The remaining 25 per cent were scattered over the other forty states. Where the states were prepared for able children, they were not afraid to discover them. In Washington an Office of Education for the Gifted and Talented was set up, directed by Dr Harold C. Lyon, Jr, to strengthen leadership in departments of education. One of the objectives was to double the number of able children being served, raising the number from 80,000 to 160,000 by 1977. There is much to be said for half-decade-long setting of objectives. Five-yearly reviews keep the progress constantly in the public mind.

The State of Connecticut had at that time fifty different programmes to broaden and deepen the education of able children. There was a Science Centre for Student Involvement, where children could undertake original investigations. At weekend and evening courses, of the many fields covered, the most popular were astronomy, geology and meteorology. One boy of eleven, in praising the centre, said there was so much apparatus that he could explore things, instead of just learning facts and figures. The State of Georgia had a course which had been running for fifteen years, part of the preliminary work which had led up to governmental acceptance. They had eighty special programmes for superior children, upon which the teacher might call, according to an individual's special interest. A Governor's Honors Program already involved 400 able children from high schools, both junior and senior. In New York City, the Bronx High School of Science, which had been started in 1938, now has 4,000 competing annually for admission. In Southern California, at Los Angeles, Dr Norman J. Mirman, who used to be President of the US National Association for Gifted Children, started a school. It began in his own house and by 1973 there were 130 children in a new school building. The Mirman School has a flexible schedule, with subjects such as Greek and electronics available. One boy of eight in this school said, 'Nobody laughs at you here for expressing an opinion; everyone has different ideas; after all, there is no one right answer to a question.'

These and many other experiments all over the United States designed to foster suitable education for the gifted and talented children are specifically encouraged now by the Washington Office. Moreover, the individual states are encouraged to seek investments by other public and private sectors in programmes for the gifted and talented. As we have seen in the British system of endowed schools, merchants and other successful business people are much more ready than we generally realise to make altruistic donations for future generations. But the Government is not in itself an organisation which can pioneer developments in new areas. A sufficient head of steam has to be worked up by people of vision for the new subject to be 'vote-catching'. Then those who would enter, or re-enter government, have to show their interest and knowledge of the subject. But, as we have also seen from our own system, one cannot just hand over ideas to the State and forget about them. The scholarship system instituted in Britain in 1893, to ensure that the brighter children had opportunity to further their studies, turned out, a century later, to be failing for several reasons: (1) the busy teacher depends on children conforming for reasons of discipline, and the bright child needs to work independently; (2) scholarship-winning was confused in the teacher's mind with hard work, and some most able children could do well without any real effort or attention; (3) bored children get up to mischief, and the teacher is liable to adopt a repressive attitude by way of punishment for inconvenience; and so on. Without doubt an appreciable percentage of able children were going on to further educational experience, but very able and divergent-thinking children who did not conform were falling by the way, 'to punish them for being naughty'. One has a hope that before very long a higher percentage of gifted original thinkers will reach high places, and the country will be governed by a higher percentage of men and women who can be both visionary and practical.

In the American search for talent, Dr Lyon states specifically, 'These children are denoted not by race, socio-economic background, ethnic origin or impaired facilities, but by their exceptional ability. They come from all levels of society, from all races and national origins, and are equally distributed between the sexes.' These are all areas where people who have succeeded *in spite* of their education are likely to give assistance, financial or otherwise, to aid the many now being lost because they cannot, despite their ability, surmount the present educational system.

Besides the Government, there is another powerful ally that is essential, and this is the university system. The highest level of research is required. We have a very long way to go in this field and might profit by a close examination of a 1973 Technical Report from California. It is by Seagoe and Mills and is entitled *UCLA Graduate Research on the Gifted and their Education*. It is part of extensive research into special education now in progress at the Graduate School of Education, University of California, Los Angeles, and the Department of Special Education, California State University, Los Angeles. The dissertations and theses reported, with two exceptions, were completed during the past fifteen years. The thirteen research projects were carried out at the Graduate School of Education at UCLA and are summarised with special emphasis on the educational needs of the gifted. Issues which emerged were: identification, early childhood education, the instructional programme, self-concept and sex role, and administration and teacher education.

The theses are all unpublished and the abstracts are produced in this form for two reasons: they are easier than the original PhD theses to read, and it is hoped that the information gained through the researches will reach a wider public in this form. The point of view taken is that gifted children have the same right to an appropriate education as other children. The social gain can only take place if the right to full development is met.

Giftedness is defined as the upper end of the normal distribution of intelligence, the highest two per cent of children, judged by ability to acquire and manipulate concepts. *Eminence* is defined as recognition by society of able people, who are often gifted. *Talent* refers to specialised ability in a limited field, such as art or music or mathematics or languages. *Creativity* is regarded as primarily a personality, rather than an intellectual factor. Creativity and giftedness are relatively independent, though the development of creativity in the gifted is important, to increase the productivity and social contribution of the intellectually able. Schools should identify children, help them to find and develop their talents, emphasise instruction which stresses problem-solving and creativity, and hope that society will recognise their contribution, thus eventually considering them eminent.

Table 7

UNPUBLISHED UCLA THESES ON GIFTED CHILDREN

Research Workers	Participants grades/years		Number subjects/controls	
Dunn (1969)	Pre-school	2–4	45	45
Walton (1961)	Kindergarten	5–6	94	88
Bowen (1969)	IV	9	20	20
Singh (1967)	V–VI	10–11	100	100
Keeling (1959)	V–VI	10–11	35	36
Fitz-Gibbon (1971)	IX	14	55	
Albers (1944)	IX Alg. I	14	17B + 15G	17B + 15G
Lessinger (1956)	Geom. I	14	17B + 15G	17B + 15G
Roberts (1960)	X–XII	15–17	45B + 19G	28B + 22G
McIntosh (1966)	Undergraduates		53	48
Wiener (1960)	Experienced teachers		200	
Mills (1973)	Male graduates*		852	
Barro (1971)	Male graduates†		20	14

* 117 Teachers of regular classes, 244 teachers of the gifted, 101 school administrators, 92 parents of gifted children, 122 community leaders, 130 members of the lay public, and 46 gifted children, all of these groups important decision-makers in the lives of gifted children.

† Male graduates working for a Master of Fine Arts Degree in Playwriting and Screenwriting.

N.B. Where there is no division into subjects, and controls, the research is into a test, or attitudes, or two approaches.

Barbara Dunn (Clark), *The Effectiveness of Teaching Selected Reading Skills to Children Two Through Four Years of Age by Television.* Unpublished EdD dissertation, UCLA, 1969.

Geneve Walton, *Identification of Intellectually Gifted Children in the Public School Kindergarten.* Unpublished EdD dissertation, UCLA, 1961.

James Joseph Bowen, *The Use of Games as an instructional Media.* Unpublished EdD dissertation, UCLA, 1969.

Surrendra Pratap Singh, *A Comparison Between Privileged Negroes, Underprivileged Negroes, Privileged Whites and Underprivileged Whites on a Test of Creativity.* Unpublished EdD dissertation, UCLA, 1967.

Janet, Keeling (Ruckert), *The Interests and Leisure Activities of Gifted Fifth and Sixth Grade Children.* Unpublished MA thesis, UCLA, 1959.

Carol Taylor Fitz-Gibbon, *An Investigation of the Advanced Progressive Matrices (1962) as a Selection Instrument for Mentally Gifted Students in Inner City Schools.* Unpublished MA thesis, UCLA, 1971.

Mary Elizabeth Alberts, *Enrichment for Superior Students in Algebra Classes.* Unpublished MA thesis, UCLA, 1944.

Leon M. Lessinger, *An Evaluation of an Enriched Program in Teaching Geometry to Gifted Students.* Unpublished EdD dissertation, UCLA, 1956.

Helen Erskine Roberts, *Factors Affecting the Academic Under-achievement of Bright High School Students.* Unpublished EdD dissertation, UCLA, 1960.

Dean Keith McIntosh, *Correlates of Self-concept in Gifted Students.* Unpublished EdD dissertation, UCLA, 1966.

Jean Lessinger Wiener, *A Study of the Relationships between Selected Variables and Attitudes of Teachers Toward Gifted Students.* Unpublished EdD dissertation, UCLA, 1960.

Barbara Nash Mills, *Attitude of Decision-making Groups Toward Gifted Children and Their School Programs.* Unpublished EdD dissertation, ULCA, 1973.

Arlene Ring Barro, *A Comparison of Two Approaches to Identifying Creativity in Graduate Student Writers.* Unpublished PhD dissertation, UCLA, 1971.

Table 7 lists the research workers according to the age of the subject with whom they worked, and gives the number of subjects and controls in each case. Below that are the names of people and theses in detail.

Many of these researchers have long experience of gifted children. All (except two now retired) have posts of high responsibility. Four are assistant professors, two are deans, two are still linked to research concerned with the study of evaluation, and so on.

It is the nature of research that the problems selected are personal to each researcher. Thus the studies reported vary widely, as they have emerged with individual students. In summarising the dissertations, Dr Mills has attempted to excerpt the findings with direct implications for educational programmes. In her summaries she seeks to answer four questions:

1 What questions of concern to programmes for the gifted was the study designed to answer, and what is the educational significance of such questions?
2 How did the investigator go about answering the question: what was the research design, what specific information was gathered, and how were the data treated?

3 What were the findings, both in relation to the question asked and in relation to other issues?

4 What does the study suggest in terms of modification or present school practices in the education of the gifted?

The accuracy of each summary was checked by the author.

May Seagoe, Professor of Education at the University of California, under whom the greater part of the work was carried out, had been a student of Terman's at Stanford University and has written his biography. She was well equipped to carry out the 'formidable task', as she herself called it, of bringing these varied postgraduate researches on gifted children together in one technical report. The basis for including a particular point in the research is that it is mentioned by three or more of the research workers. She herself is the first to admit that such a system could miss important points, since most important discoveries may well be made by just one highly perceptive research worker. However, every basis for selection has some defect and this appears to have less defects than others; and even this one demanded bold and hazardous interpretational leaps. She found five recurring groups of suggestions emerging from the research, and treats each of them in turn.

The first group is *identification*. The identification of pre-school gifted children presents serious problems. Nomination by the teachers proved grossly inadequate at the kindergarten stage, and might well be replaced by group testing, followed by individual examination. Sometimes the problem of identification can be bypassed by using other methods of selecting presumably talented children. A definite diagnostic process must be found for those who, on school entry, are capable of learning more difficult material. In secondary school, group testing is insufficient for identifying the gifted, and particularly the highly gifted. It also misses the under-achievers and the gifted in the Black community. Even the pattern of creativity differs in the two cultures. Less emphasis should be put on the results of a single test. Case evaluation should include individual testing, observation in the case of both young and older children, and the measurement of special abilities and interests for the older children. Laborious though this may be, it is the way to select the children and provide them with a suitable programme.

The second group is *early childhood education*. Ideally the children should be identified in early childhood or at the latest in the first two or three years of school. During those years the personality, including creativity, is still flexible, emerging talents can be encouraged and directed, and acceleration can profitably take place. Early experience of a programme suited to the gifted is critical. Those who are almost able to teach themselves reading by about three years could very likely profit from television as a medium for learning to read. Another possibility is early entrance to kindergarten or primary school, with enriched individual programmes. States in America which have arranged such early entrance have found it highly successful. If a gifted child can reduce his time in school by one to four years, he gains that much more time for productive work, and is that much less frustrated by conventional schooling. This second group, on early childhood education, strongly recommends that California gives high priority to establishing a plan for early school entrance for gifted children.

The third group is the *instructional process*. Though much has gone into programmes and material for the gifted, there is general discontent with these programmes on the part of the gifted themselves. The negative attitude may stem in part from social rejection by the peer group and the school community. But the possibility that the cause is within the special programmes needs vigorous exploration. The gifted are a varied group, in ability, in interests and in talents. Thus the programme must be highly individualised. The focus should be on the development of the diverse talents and abilities of each child. This is particularly true of the most highly gifted of all, who, apart from their diverse talents, are conceptually so very far ahead of their contemporaries. The programme should allow continuous and unlimited potential for growth, individualised and non-coercive, rich in resources of materials and persons, jointly planned by teachers, parents and students. Open education may be the structural model, with attention given to transfer (change in ability), problem-solving, creativity and the development of attitudes. There should be more

mature, wide-ranging scientific reading, and use of games as a
method of instruction, to promote social interaction as well as
achievement. Criteria for the selection of content are essential.
More work is no answer. The capacities of the gifted children
should dictate the content.

Thus the role of the teacher is different, stimulating concentration and thoughtfulness, through reflecting back questions and
stimulating him to seek the answers himself. In this way the child
reasons inductively from observed data, instead of generalising
from other people's information. A classroom climate which
maximises creativity is stimulated by specialised technical reading,
use of sketches and diagrams, use of self-directed questions, and so
on. Parenthetically, one might point out that Burt, in the joint
British-American publication, The Year Book of Education, *The
Gifted Child* (1962) was criticising current thinking along the
same lines. He pointed out that we were failing to discover or
develop the potential of these children by laying too much stress
on *reproductive* and *analytical* thinking while undervaluing
synthetic and *creative* thinking. The Californian research report,
concerning instructional processes, goes on to say that such a
creative climate as described will stimulate concentration and
thoughtfulness. So far schools have stressed the intellectual side at
the expense of creativity. If they accept the importance of
creativity, then they must offer opportunity for independent work.
There are also recommendations concerning minority groups, such
as low socio-economic groups and ethnic groups, which should be
carefully studied by those who are experts in watching for gifted
children here. Their level of aspiration, even plans for continuing
school, have to be raised; parental interest has to be awakened.
Where such work was carried out, results were even greater than
with more normal groups.

The fourth group is *self-concept and sex role*. Previous studies
draw attention to the relatively mature personality of gifted children. Yet this is not how it seems to the gifted themselves, who
tend to have a much lower self-concept than the less able. As a
result they are less productive than they might be. Even special
programmes do not seem to help. The longer the gifted have been
on special programmes, the lower their self-concept seems to be.

They need more encouragement, emphasis on strengths, and success in the eyes of other children to improve their self-concept. We all feel more at ease with persons who share our interests; gifted children are no exception. That is why they enjoy the company of other gifted children, older children, or adults; but members of their age group reject difference categorically, particularly during adolescence. So the gifted hide their difference. Thus there is a need, not only for differentiated programmes for the gifted in academic fields, but also for school-wide programmes which cut across a wide range of ages and abilities, to bring together diverse individuals in tasks where special talents and social learnings are important, and where there are problem-solving tasks to be done.

Another finding in this area of self-concept and sex role, of considerable importance, is that for girls the problem of social acceptance is acute. Full acceptance for the girls means not only acceptance by children of their own age but also by children and adults of both sexes, despite the fact that their interests and abilities will violate culturally accepted norms as well. Here is a clear example of where society has to change its attitude. Teachers have to help the children of normal ability to be more tolerant of the gifted amongst them; for this the teachers have to disengage the virtue of strenuous effort from exceptionally high ability, so that the gifted and the average can each feel accepted for themselves.

All who work towards reasonable change in society have to help everyone to recognise the long-standing misapprehension concerning the socially accepted norms for girls. The regions of activity open to girls have to be greatly widened; otherwise the struggle to break through to spheres of work which interest them is too great, and can harm personality development. As we should have expected, these researches demonstrate that gifted girls show more maladjustment and need for counselling than girls of average ability. Naturally influenced by the out-dated notions of the society in which they live, when selecting careers they set themselves lower standards than their high ability warrants. Like all normal people, they wish to be accepted by society and are therefore forced to compromise, accepting lower standards for themselves than they are capable of achieving. A way has to be found to interweave special programmes for the gifted with the life of school. This is the only way to help the exceptionally able girls to gain confidence by being accepted, while learning to accept themselves in what we now find is their true sex role.

The last group concerns *administration and teacher education*. There is a clear need for change in the preparation of teachers of the gifted, in pre-service and in-service education of teachers of normal classrooms, and school administrators, and in public relations programmes with the community at large. A varied approach to understanding the gifted is called for. Teachers have to be carefully selected and specifically prepared. They should have reasonably high scholastic aptitude and personal stability. They need help in understanding how the gifted learn, in maximising problem-solving and creativity, and in stimulating interest in programmes designed for the gifted.

Teachers and administrators in regular classrooms also need help in developing greater understanding of the gifted, both in preparation for their work and by in-service education. In this way they can effectively participate, support differentiated instruction, and promote activities that will increase acceptance of the gifted by the peer group. Such modifications will positively affect public relations. Many schools cannot start programmes because of lack of support. This is particularly so where there are large populations of low socio-economic status, and ethnic minorities. In addition to more formal presentations, adults in the community should be enlisted through voluntary work, and in participation in projects serving common interests. Only when unfavourable attitudes are changed to favourable ones will the gifted children themselves be content.

There are now other research findings on gifted and talented children coming from universities in other areas of the United States, but few can rival this impressive collation of postgraduate work over a long period. It is no surprise that the work of Lewis M. Terman was first recognised in the State of California, since his monumental team researches on gifted children emanated from there. The report leaves us in no doubt that a multi-level campaign lies ahead. The ablest children of the last eighteen centuries in the

British Isles have all too often known very unhappy times, been subjected to outdated methods of teaching, sometimes to flagrant cruelty, to total neglect in the case of able girls, and to repression of creative thinking. Today, more than ever, they need profound understanding, not only for their own sakes, but for the sake of society and the future.

Bibliography

Artists Now, *Patronage of the Creative Artist* (London: 107 Arlington Road NW1, 1974).

Ashcroft, Peggy (to David Jones) in *Great Acting*, Hal Burton (ed.) (London: BBC Publications, 1966).

Association of Headmistresses, *Reluctant Revolutionaries* (London: Pitman, 1974).

Binet, A., *L'Étude Experimental de l'Intellect* (Paris: Schleicher, 1903).

Bridges, S. A., *Gifted Children and the Brentwood Experiment* (London: Pitman, 1969).

Bronowski, J., *Science and Human Values* (London: Pelican, 1958).

Burt, C. L., 'The experimental study of general intelligence', *British Journal of Psychology*, 3 (1909).

——, 'Intelligence and social mobility', *British Journal of Statistical Psychology*, XIV, 1 (1961).

——, 'The gifted child', *British Journal of Statistical Psychology*, XIV, 2 (1961).

See also Year Book of Education, *The Gifted Child* and Pringle, M. K., *Able Misfits*.

Buxton Forman, M. (ed.), *The Letters of John Keats* (London: OUP, 1947).

Cozens, A., 'A new method of assisting the invention in original drawing compositions of landscapes' (1785?), see Oppé.

Day, A., 'The nation's wealth: who owns it?', *Observer* (20 January 1974).

Diringer, D., *Writing* (London: Thames Hudson, 1962).

Gardner, B., *The Public Schools* (London: Hamish Hamilton, 1973).

Gombrich, E. H., *Symbolic Images. Studies in the art of the renaissance* (London: Phaidon, 1972).

Graves, R., *The White Goddess* (London: Faber & Faber, 1948).

Kerlouégan, F., 'Le Latin du *De Excidio Britanniae* de Gildas' in *Christianity in Britain 300–700*, M. W. Barley and R. P. C. Hanson (eds) (Leicester: LUP, 1968).

Lorenz, K., *King Solomon's Ring* (London: Methuen, 1952).

Lowenfeld, M., *Creative and Mental Growth* (London: Collier-Macmillan, 1966).

Mercouri, M., *I Was Born Greek* (London: Hodder & Stoughton, 1971).

Naumann, A., *Poems: Now has my summer* (London: Collins, 1966).

Oppé, A. P., *Alexander and John Robert Cozens* (London: A. & C. Black , 1952.

Percival, A. C., *The Origins of the Headmasters' Conference* (London: Murray, 1969).

Plowden Report, *Children and Their Primary Schools* (London: HMSO, 1967.

Pringle, M. K., *Able Misfits* (London: Longman, 1970).

Read, H., *The Meaning of Art* (London: Faber & Faber, 1931).

Redcliffe-Maud Report, *Reform of Local Government in England* (London: HMSO, 1970)

Rowlands, P., *Gifted Children and Their Problems* (London: Dent, 1974).

Seagoe, M. V. and Mills, B. N., *UCLA Graduate Research on the Gifted and Their Education*, Technical Report (SERP 1973–A6, Graduate School of Education, University of California, Los Angeles, 1973).

Solzhenitsyn, A., *One Word of Truth . . .*, BBC Russian Service Members (tr.) (London: Bodley, 1970).

Steiner, G., *In Bluebeard's Castle. Some notes towards the re-definition of culture* (London: Faber & Faber, 1971).

Tempest, N. R. *Teaching Clever Children* London: Routledge & Kegan Paul, 1974).

Terman, L. M. and Merrill, M. A., *Stanford-Binet Intelligence Scale*, 1st British edn (London: Harrap, 1961).

Whitaker's Almanack, Shorter Edn, Census of Population, 1971 (London: 1973).

Year Book of Education, *The Gifted Child* (London and New York, in association with the Teachers' College, Columbia University, New York and the Institute of Education, London University; London: Evans, 1962).

INDEX